DOCTOR
IN AN
OLD WORLD

By permission Overseas Missionary Fellowship, Philadelphia, Pa.

DOCTOR
IN AN
OLD WORLD

The Story of Robert Earl Beddoe
Medical Missionary to China

HELEN THAMES RALEY

WORD BOOKS

Waco, Texas ━ London, England

Because he suggested, encouraged, and inspired
the writing of the Beddoe story
and because he shared my happiness
for its publication
Doctor in an Old World
is lovingly dedicated to

John Wesley Raley
1902–1968
who made all my dreams come true

Acknowledgements

—◆—

Many people wrote this book.

First of all, I should like to express gratitude to the Beddoe family

Mrs. Robert E. Beddoe

Mrs. Addie Buckner Beddoe Choate

Mrs. Mary Frances Beddoe Ross

who shared correspondence, scrapbooks, memorabilia and, of course, the memories.

It was Dr. Cal Guy, Professor of Missions, Southwestern Baptist Theological Seminary, who, in an article for *The Baptist Standard*, gave me the idea in the first place, then read a possible first chapter.

Miss Wanda Jones, OBU student, typed the manuscript, and her proficiency stood me in good stead with the editors and publishers.

Miss Mary Ruth Howes, born in China of missionary parents, is responsible for the careful editing of this manuscript. (Providentially, I think, she became associated with Word Books just when I needed her.)

To Mr. and Mrs. Randall Spears, Ardmore, Oklahoma, delightful traveling companions, I want to express a special love and gratitude for the stimulation, the sparkle, the added dimension of interest and concern with which they shared our modern missionary journey.

Helen Raley

Of Music, Medicine, and Missions.

History recounts that priests of the early tribes were also the "medicine men" of their groups. Furthermore, the priest-healers frequently utilized music in their worship and other services.

The true physician regards himself as God's minister of health. Like the clergyman, he answers the divine call to serve mankind in selfless continuing devotion. The real musician has a sensitive spirit of communion with God, with himself and with others, and music has a definite therapeutic value.

Therefore, the acme of service should be rendered by a Christian physician who is also a real musician. Such a man was Robert E. Beddoe, M.D.—superbly trained in music in his younger years, then answering the scientific and humanistic challenge of medicine, and ultimately devoting his tremendous talents to serving as a medical missionary in China.

In the fifty centuries of recorded history, medical science, by the grace of God has made tremendous advances to almost undreamed of accomplishments, such as transplantation of human organs. But the one characteristic that has never been superseded, is the deep concern for humanity as the true physician devotes his skill and understanding to the individual patient, meeting the needs of those he serves in the spirit of the Great Physician.

Dr. Robert E. Beddoe was a pioneer medical missionary of Southern Baptists to the tremendous land of China. The political misfortunes of that Oriental colossus kept him from realizing his ultimate dreams, but he was truly one of the greatest Christian heroes of the ages.

And now a gifted author, Mrs. Helen Raley, with many personal ties with the Robert Beddoe family, has brought out the thrilling and inspiring story of "music, medicine, and missions" in her book *Doctor in an Old World.* It deserves an immediate place in every family and church library, as well as every medical library.

MILFORD O. ROUSE, M.D.
Immediate Past President
American Medical Association

PREFACE

—◆—

During strenuous days of wartime China, I saw Robert E. Beddoe in action. He was a towering personality and a creative force in the missionary undertaking.

As a surgeon, he had high reputation both in his own country and on the mission field. He delighted in his professional practice until eye difficulties made surgery impossible. His remarkable administrative talents were brought to bear upon the work of the Stout Memorial Hospital in such a manner that the loss occasioned by his inability to practice surgery was offset by his outstanding record in hospital administration. The hospital was known widely throughout South China and patients came to it from far and near.

While greatly concerned for high professional standards and efficiency in hospital administration, he was even more concerned about the spiritual ministry of the institution for which he was responsible. Ably assisted by his wife in the religious program of the hospital, he maintained a strong staff of qualified Chinese Christian 'workers to minister to the spiritual needs of all patients who came to the hospital.

His accomplishments as an organist and pianist brought delight to gatherings of his fellow missionaries. His administrative qualities caused the Foreign Mission Board to turn to him as acting secretary for the work in China during the days when the Secretary for the Orient was first immobilized in a Japanese concentration camp and then was repatriated to the United States. He assumed responsibilities with firmness and clarity during difficult days of inflation, war emergencies and uncertainty.

In order to be in better communication with the entire war-time mission, he moved from Wuchow to Kweilin. With the coming of the United States 14th Air Force, a large number of American servicemen soon were frequent visitors at the mission. Open house was maintained each week for servicemen and one of the highlights of the gatherings consisted of singing to the accompaniment of Robert E. Beddoe at the piano.

Two of us who were ministers at the mission served as civilian chaplains at the air base. Dr. Beddoe was always ready to participate with his music and good fellowship.

He had a comprehensive view of the missionary task. He saw the place of a high quality medical institution standing not as an end in itself, but as a major factor in Christian witness to people who needed not only healing for their bodies, but spiritual help as well. His concern for the welfare of the churches and the preaching and teaching of the Christian message held high place in his heart.

He was a man of sterling Christian character, deep convictions and strong determination to make his service as meaningful for the cause of his Master as could be done. He set high standards in his own life and looked for high standards in others. He was a remarkable missionary. He was respected and beloved by those who knew him, and brought encouragement and strength to his fellow workers.

The story of his life will bring blessing to all who read it. We are indebted to the author for her work of love in presenting this splendid book to people who cherish the cause of missions and admire heroic service wherever it is found.

BAKER JAMES CAUTHEN
Executive Secretary
Foreign Mission Board
Southern Baptist Convention

Contents

◆

FOREWORD

A Modern Missionary Journey

◆

When I was a little girl, I often wondered and worried about the strange people in foreign lands who were a deep concern of my mother's Missionary Aid Society. Then, I had no way of knowing that the cozy, safe world of my childhood would ever be affected by events in China, or Japan, or Africa—those faraway places in my Sunday school songs. There seemed to be much interest in China, but I was too young to understand the extent of mission enterprises already well established in such centers as Shanghai, Canton, Teng-chow, or to know that Texas was well represented along the heavily populated tributaries of the Pearl River. Certainly, I could not foresee that the world of my maturity would be the result of on-the-spot history, the shifting and sorting of daily events broadcast to the most remote spots of our shrunken globe.

In today's world, one goes so far, so fast.

Little did I realize then, when Dr. Raley and I, accompanied by Mr. and Mrs. Randall Spears of Ardmore, Oklahoma, boarded a plane at Oklahoma City's Will Rogers Airport the morning of July 1, 1963, that the next twenty days would provide the most dramatic experience of my life—and life on the Oklahoma Baptist University campus has been far from provincial. I had no idea that this short

missionary journey to the Far East would provoke my thinking into a compulsion to write down some of the unrecorded
history of my time, nor that my missions perspective would
become so sensitive to the people and places of those few
busy days. Suddenly, I was aware of a continuity, a sort of
chain reaction, the never-ending effects of good will on the
earth. It was then that I remembered my mother's concern,
my childhood worry about "the little children, all the children of the world. . . ." The missionary enterprise about
which I had read all my life was no longer an abstract and
ethereal dream; rather, it became a pattern of person-to-
person, a living link in one of the great Godward movements
of history.

As the plane headed west across the Oklahoma plains, I
checked all the necessities of world travel which crowded my
hand satchel. There it was, tucked in safely, a faded photograph. In the pale yellowed brown of the years, I could see
a dozen or so Chinese figures posing in front of a squarish,
white, stucco building, the Southern Baptist Hospital in
Wuchow, South China. Two Americans stood in the center.
Written across the back of the picture, which was to become
an introduction to many groups in Hong Kong, were questions of identification, some notes, some dates. On this little
Stanley-Livingston safari, I represented the bureau of missing
persons. "Do you remember anyone in this picture?" "Who
is this?" "Do you have news of him?" "When did you see her
last?" "Is the building still there?"

From these questions and subsequent conversations, a
story came to life—a story that had to be written. For that
little picture returned safely to the treasured scrapbook and
the remembering heart of my cherished friend, Mrs. Robert
E. Beddoe, the elegant missionary-emerita of another era,
whose life through a strange destiny has become a part of
mine and a living legend across the South.

In retrospect Louella Beddoe relives the life and work of

her husband, Dr. Robert Earl Beddoe of Texas, one of the most colorful figures of Baptist history and of modern missionary effort. His medical-missionary career spanned turbulent years of Chinese history. Those years I, too, remember— years crowded with explosive events and national crises: World War I, depression, Pearl Harbor, World War II, and all the sociological aftermath of a torn-apart world. I remember, too, the busy preoccupation of our personal lives: Dr. Raley's thirty years of building OBU, denominational promotion, the children's growing up, their careers, the frustrating adjustment to a "new world." Somewhere in all the busyness of these years, there has been a vacuum of missionary facts. Where are the hero stories, choice reading of another generation? Lost in the tremendous avalanche of post-war writing and publishing is the interest and inspiration once given by the biographies of Livingstone, Carey, Miss Lottie Moon, and countless other stalwarts of the missionary crusade. In the contemporary exploitation of a tasteless, lawless society, such volumes of significance are all too few or hidden. Our world is a sophisticated, knowledgeable one, with little inclination to discover the personal destiny, the human touch with which Divine Providence directs ideas, thoughts, dreams, so great, so small—so far-reaching, but with love abounding.

We were on our way home from the Far East. Tucked into the same bag, now grown bulkier and more travel-worn, was the returning photograph and a tiny, tissue-wrapped gift directed and inscribed to Mrs. Beddoe—a bit of carved ivory set into a delicately designed brooch—"With love from Lillian and David Wong." In another world, in another time, David's father was in that picture, an associate of the Beddoes of Wuchow. Young David, now a prominent architectural engineer in Hong Kong, had been told of the American missionary couple; but somehow time and circumstances had all but erased the memory, retrieved now through a faded photograph in a tourist's purse.

A strange coincidence further developed my interest in writing this volume. Upon our return to Shawnee, Dr. Raley and I sat in our usual places at the First Baptist Church for the next Sunday morning service. To be there in our pew, home and safe, after having flown the vast Pacific, was a reflection of unbelievable wonder and of profound thankfulness. Enveloped in a peaceful glory and in the soft sweetness of the organ prelude, I recognized the familiar cadences of Bach's "Jesu, Joy of Man's Desiring," and thought how perfectly arranged were the orchid chrysanthemums there on the altar—the same shade as those I had enjoyed in the Orient. Then I found the brief note in the bulletin: "The altar flowers today are in loving remembrance of the birthday of Dr. Robert E. Beddoe by Mrs. Beddoe and their daughters."

After the service, Mrs. Beddoe was the first to greet us. After all, we had been in the country, and she was eager for some word, for some brief comment on "How are things there?" And then, just to me, she said, "Helen, wasn't it beautiful—the Bach? It was the last piece Dr. Beddoe ever played. Isn't it interesting that the organist chose it on his day?"

I knew that the Beddoe story had to be told—at least, to Southern Baptists, whom he represented in China during the critical years of wars, depression, and economic disaster. Because of his contribution to the great stream of missionary effort, his identification with America-China relations, and his stature in the professional world, he achieved a rare immortality among Baptist missionary greats. Humbly and gratefully I present *Doctor in an Old World,* a biographical story of a gallant Albert Schweitzer of another continent, whose "magnificent obsessions"—music, medicine, and missions—honor his memory and his work for God.

1

"I Listened to His Music"

"FAITH is not an argument."

The doctor spoke slowly, weighing each word as though he needed them more to reassure himself than to convince the young Air Force major who faced him.

"It is not a debate. It is an experience. It is not easy to see all this swept away—church, missionary work, medical work. I can only have faith that eventually there shall arise an even greater concept of God's Kingdom here in China . . . not for me to see, perhaps. I am too old to begin over again. But there will be others to carry on where we have left off."

"Sir, I wish I had some of that faith. How does one get the hang of it?" Frank Otte asked the lean, slight figure standing there in his wrinkled medic whites, his tired eyes squinting toward the far-off sky where Texas was, his shoulders stooped from the long days of never-ending work and anguish. "Somehow I have missed that kind of faith."

It was January, 1943. A contingent of the Flying Tigers trained under the command of General Claire Chennault, USAF, had arrived in Kweilin, South China. This assignment, listed as "top secret," involved espionage, counter-espionage, and other varied duties of an Intelligence section. Major Frank R. Otte, USAF, had come to Kweilin six months earlier to arrange facilities for the Fighter and Bomber Squadrons and the Chinese civilian staff.

Two worlds were writhing in the horrible holocaust of war—the East and the West.

In the broadcasts were names like the Solomons, the Coral Sea, and Midway in the South Pacific, where the American Navy and marines were vulnerable to heavy fire from Japanese bombers and sniping operations through infested jungles. February 1943 would see the Guadalcanal campaign finally end in American victory. Later that spring General Douglas MacArthur would be given strategic command of all south and southwest Pacific areas.

Also in the news was the appointment of Major General Dwight D. Eisenhower as commander-in-chief of all Allied Forces in Africa. At Casablanca, President Roosevelt and Mr. Churchill would meet with their chiefs-of-staff to plan the coming invasion of Sicily and the air operations over Europe. The Tunisian campaign had been a costly step toward victory. With the severe Russian winter taking toll of men and machines, there would be weeks of bitter fighting over Stalingrad. It would be a long road—and another spring—to Normandy.

Like flames of fire, war encircled the world—a great conflagration on one side setting off inflammable incidents on the other. China lay in the path. But China had been in the throes of war long before Pearl Harbor. By 1943 Kwangsi Province had become a teeming refugee camp with hundreds of thousands crushing into every city, pouring over the countryside, hunting cover anywhere from the advancing forces and the war in the sky.

It was said to be the largest migration of people, both foreign and Chinese, in the history of the world—this great swarm of human misery which surged ahead of the Japanese

offensive. Rushed from their homes, with what few posses-
sions they could gather quickly and carry with them, they
trudged along, dragging and supporting the old, the sick, the
young. With their starving children and hopeless aged, the
blind leading the blind along the dusty roads, the miserable
trek of humanity never stopped.

Because of the war, Kweilin was the headquarters for the
Southern Baptist work in China. Headquarters had been
established under Dr. M. Theron Rankin, but he was now
confined by the Japanese in Stanley Prison, Hong Kong. At
the request of the Foreign Mission Board in Richmond,
Virginia, Dr. Robert E. Beddoe had left his medical work
as superintendent of Stout Memorial Hospital in Wuchow
and moved to Kweilin. Dr. William Wallace took over the
duties at the hospital in Wuchow. Dr. Beddoe assumed responsibility for the work, the care, and the safety of the
Southern Baptist personnel in South China.

At Kweilin were Dr. Nichols, Miss Hattie Stallings, and Dr.
and Mrs. Baker James Cauthen and their children, as well as
the Beddoes. In addition to the local Baptist Church and a
theological school, the compound was temporarily housing
Pooi Ching and Pooi To Baptist Schools—elementary and
high school level students and teachers, who had been evacuated from enemy territory in Canton. In and around Kweilin,
Baptists had also established medical and clinical services.
Later, the students and teachers were evacuated by boat up
the Foo River and tributaries, evading the Japanese on their
way to Chungking, capital of Free China.

And more refugees kept coming. For many, the only place
of hope and help was the refugee center adjacent to the
Baptist Mission compound. Here free medical treatment was
available. The missionary personnel rallied to a man, attend-
ing the sick, the hungry, those who could not live. Sanitary
conditions created a crisis; medical supplies and food ran
short; all Christian literature was soon gone.

As the war inched closer, thousands more refugees found shelter in nearby caves. At the same time, the tremendous drain on the city market presented an insoluble problem to both the city authorities and the administrators of the mission.

"Some days I can hardly stand up under the strain," Dr. Beddoe wrote during this time; "these suffering people, and our suffering co-missionaries—the strain breaks out in the most unaccountable times and ways. Some days back I was walking in the rain on muddy, filthy paths after sending a cablegram home. My heart was bleeding as I thought of recent events. I passed a woman and a little girl, eight or nine years old. The child was dressed in a few rags and an old coat. She was as thin as a sparrow. The weather was cold, and she was drawn together against the wind and rain. She carried a small basket, and I noticed her picking up bits of straw, chewings from sugar cane, tiny bits of bamboo, and so forth, for fuel. To keep up with her mother she had to travel in a slow trot. Yet there was a smile on her drawn face, and she glanced at me as at a friend and said, 'American gentleman, friend of China.' Well, the whole picture just broke my heart. I thought of my little girls. In a flash, their sheltered lives passed before my mind's eye. I thought, 'What if that were my daughter?' Without volition, the tears streamed from my eyes and I stopped in the rain and the wind, leaning against a machine gun pill-box and wept. O God in heaven, how can we stand it?"

This was war, war that had begun as early as 1931, creeping stealthily over the Manchurian horizon, through chinks in the Great Wall, to burst into full force in 1937. This was the war that stalked with bands of roving, ravaging bandits across the vast land of 450,000,000 people, leaving like locusts of atrocities a trail of murdered, tortured, and starving. Unsuspected, then ignored, this was the war that burst with the flame of its "rising sun" over the serene ships in the calm, blue harbor at Honolulu.

And in America, the school children had gathered up scrap iron and bits of metal to send to Japan! And with those countless carloads of junk there had flowed a steady stream of American petroleum products to Tokyo, Yokohama, and Osaki!

Madame Chiang Kai-shek had appealed for help in that unforgettable, liquid voice, softly southern and slurred: "Tell me, is the silence of the Western nations in the face of such massacres, such demolition of homes, a sign of the triumph of civilization with its humanitarianism, its code of conduct, its chivalry, and its claims of Christian influence?"

Into the already crowded conditions in Kweilin came the contingent of the 14th USAF for whom Major Otte was responsible. But there was no place for them to go, no place to set up technical installations and housing for men and materiel of the U.S. government. That is, there was none until Texas medic Dr. Robert E. Beddoe, gaunt and weary and heartsick of war, opened the gate for makeshift USAF headquarters to be established on the Southern Baptist mission compound.

As interpreter and senior advisor, Dr. Beddoe was ever helpful in the daily solution of problems involving Chinese etiquette and military protocol. Often he would drop in for a bedroom-office chat with the men in the little bungalow. Easy and friendly, warm and understanding, he was completely relaxed with the officers and men of the base, always heartened by American voices, news from the States, and the latest word from home. For one who had lived outside the United States since he was a very young man, here was a special camaraderie.

Such a group was described by Rex Ray after he, Dr. Beddoe, and the young Dr. Cauthen had visited with some of the young American flyers. They are "living specimens," he said, "of what United States sunshine, food, and health can make of God's creatures called men. Compared to these rosy-cheeked boys, we look like a crew of bloodless ghosts."

As the Japanese pressed farther south and west, Kweilin became a goal and a stopping place for missionaries from other points in China. The mission administration on the compound handled the complex details necessary for keeping in touch with the Foreign Mission Board in Richmond, Virginia. For missionaries, Kweilin was their last glimpse of China. They never returned to their stations, for they were flown out the back door and "over the hump" into India by Major Otte's men, in one of the most dramatic evacuation movements of the war. After one flight word came through that Mrs. Beddoe and some of the other missionaries were safe at the Indian border. Southern Baptists were indeed beating a solemn retreat, but only to plan advance strategy.

Dr. Beddoe did not leave with his wife, but stayed to look after the many local properties of the mission and to do what he could to alleviate human suffering. For many weary weeks, he lived with his aloneness and anguish for the plight of the homeless. At each day's end came the book work, the files of reports, the coded communications. If only his eyes could hold out. It was when he was most exhausted that he played the piano—always late at night. Nothing could so assuage weariness like playing some favorite hymns, some old hit tunes of younger days, perhaps a theme from a remembered classic. Even after thirty-five years of hard work in and for China, his doctor's hands, his skilled fingers, kept their touch and technique to manipulate difficult passages. Occasionally, he would improvise on some almost-gone melody.

Major Otte remembers "the holly hedge which surrounded his compound home. Many, many nights I stood there and listened to his music. Robert never knew this, nor the many times the tears dew-dropped down my cheeks for I, too—with a wife and children many thousands of miles away—could also be desperately lonely."

Occasionally, when food was not too scarce, Dr. Beddoe

would come over to the cottage headquarters for dinner with the boys. When he said the blessing, he blessed them all. On such occasions, it was like a miniature United Nations— Americans in and out of uniform, Chinese, Eurasian, Portuguese, White Russians. Usually, the conversation was superior to the food.

Eventually, the orders came to evacuate everyone, baggage limited to thirty-five pounds per person. Again, it was Major Otte's responsibility. The final rounds were made to dispose of what was left—china and crystal in the cupboard, a few pieces of furniture, some linens, the books—and the piano.

Perhaps a more unusual document was never drawn up.

The entire Baptist mission, with all its buildings and all effects, was turned over to the 14th USAF contingent and to Major Otte—in trust, to do whatever was deemed necessary.

"This strange transfer of property from a church organization to the United States, at that time, appeared necessary," the Major wrote in retrospect. "The Chinese Nationalists were in the turmoils of defeat. Local officials had already made efforts to 'restore' the missionary facilities to their 'rightful owners,' the Chinese. In the face of such uncertainties, we mutually agreed it safer to deed the properties to the United States; and, if victory permitted, we assumed that later the United States would return these properties to the Southern Baptist Mission."

Thus the document was duly signed by Dr. Robert E. Beddoe, representing the Mission, by Major Frank R. Otte, representing the U.S. Air Force, and by the local American Consul, representing the State Department. On September 4, 1944, Dr. Beddoe made one last request of his American flyer-friend as they jeeped toward the air base, "Major, don't let them get my piano. Destroy it if you must, but don't let them get it." Then he was off for the homeland—to Texas.

The next few days were dangerous and desperate. On

September 8, all citizens were ordered to leave the city; on the 9th, all Air Force personnel. On the 10th, the city was on fire, the Chinese carrying out a "scorched earth" policy. In the late afternoon of the 11th, the final USAF contingents retreated by air to other bases—and that night demolition crews totally destroyed every identification of USAF in Kweilin. Later, the Japanese attacked; the Chinese retreated.

Many months after the war, Dr. Beddoe returned to Kweilin; from there he wrote to Major Otte: "Remember that large rock deeply embedded right in front of the mission house? That alone remains. There is nothing left to give testimony of many missionary years in Kwangsi Province. I sat there and wept."

Through all the tragic vicissitudes of war and its aftermath, Christian faith declared that the great missionary and philanthropic movements dedicated to "good will toward men" are only slowed down—they never stop. Indeed, "though weeping may endure for the night, joy cometh in the morning." The work of Dr. Beddoe and his valiant associates was not in vain. Though the seed lies dormant and the plants seem weak and overrun, the flowering will come. That kind of faith, all too rare, is found in odd, unlikely places—in a war-ravaged city or at a lonely post of duty, in a jolting jeep or in the "wild blue yonder" of the USAF, in the nighttime sounds of a missionary compound or in the imminent countdowns of this space age.

"Yes," the Major writes, "I took care of the piano, but well remembered are those far-eastern evenings when I listened to his music."

There is a story to be told. . . .

2

From Texas to China

FROM Kentucky, to be pastor of the First Baptist Church of Paris, Texas, a young preacher came in 1861. In Paris Robert Cooke Buckner began a ministry of many facets: preaching, writing, and organizing benevolences throughout this pioneer country. All too soon he became involved in the war effort, for across the Mississsippi the straggling shades of blue and gray brought the nation's division to the west. Some of the skirmishes fought in Texas were among the most critical battles of the Civil War.

To answer the desperate calls for food, clothing, and supplies for the soldiers, Buckner helped the women in the Paris church organize a Ladies' Sewing Circle, which later inspired the beginning of a new meeting-house and began the far-reaching enterprises of Baptist women in our time. In 1867, the society reported sending money to the General Association for Missions in Indian Territory. The idea spread to Dallas, where in 1872, a similar organization earned $500.00 to become the foundation of the First Baptist Church of Dallas. Eventually interest in women's groups as a vital part of each church spread all across the South. Today, the national organization of women is one of the world's most powerful groups, the Woman's Missionary Union, Auxiliary to the Southern Baptist Convention.

By 1880, Robert Buckner was president of the Baptist General Association of Texas. He served in that capacity through the Association's merging with the Baptist General Convention of Texas. Elected president of the Convention again in 1893, he served for twenty consecutive history-making years. At the same time, his gifted writings in religious and denominational periodicals began to promote his dream of caring for orphan children, and aroused Texas Baptists to share in his concern.

Many remember the patriarchal figure of this preacher in the last years of his life—the presence of this great and good man, who cared about homeless children. The kind grandfather eyes and long gray beard belied his strength and energy. Father Buckner's heart was so big that it not only encircled all the children of Texas, but "all the children of the world." For those who lived inside the Great Wall of China, where by then his grandson was a missionary-doctor, he cared in a special way. Everywhere he went, from every pulpit, he asked the little children, looking down toward those who sat on the front row, to save their "buffalo nickels" and pennies to help care for the orphans of the world. Many a coin was dropped proudly in red-velvet lined offering plates, or perhaps in a man's panama hat in summer outdoor meetings.

Robert Buckner had opened his Buckner's Orphan's Home in 1880 with three children in a rented cottage. In 1881 it moved to its present location in East Dallas, which was then far out in the country and somewhat inaccessible. "He built the institution at a cost of much personal sacrifice, and he so endeared the institution to his brethren that its future is secure." [1] The home is known the world over, a magnificent

---

[1] *Centennial Story of Texas Baptists*

monument to a great and good man who cared, while the rushing world passes by on a six-lane thoroughfare, known as Buckner Boulevard.

From one generation to another, the torch is passed. If Addie Buckner Beddoe had not had a name familiar to all Texas Baptists, she would have made one for herself. She was the daughter of Robert Cooke Buckner and a sister to Hal and Joe Buckner, co-managers with their father of Buckner's Orphan's Home. Hal became a missionary to China; Joe became a preacher. Addie married Dr. Albert F. Beddoe, an ordained minister and a doctor of medicine; she was the mother of Albert Beddoe, Baptist minister, and Dr. Robert E. Beddoe, medical missionary to China.

Addie Buckner Beddoe was elected secretary of Texas Woman's Missionary Union in March, 1911, and served until 1923. She was determined to expand missionary interest among women in the Baptist churches. Impressively capable and attractive, she traveled out of Dallas via the new inter-urban, inspiring women with her speaking and writing to identify themselves with the fast-growing Baptist work. For distant meetings and conventions she traveled by train, and always with a steamer trunk to be "checked through"; the same trunk was used years later by granddaughters going off to college. For seventeen years she was also associated with her father in the work of the Home where her husband was principal of the school. By then her doctor-son was absorbed in the ministry of the Stout Memorial Hospital in Wuchow, China.

Albert Beddoe was a pioneer Dallas physician who shared his wife's concern over needs both at home and abroad. He was a co-founder of the Baylor University College of Medicine and was a preacher too. Associated for many years with Buckner Orphan's Home, he was known for countless charities, as well as for his fine professional practice. Because of the tragic and unnecessary death of one of his children due to lack of medical knowledge, Dr. Beddoe became interested in the new field of pediatrics, the care and prevention of childhood diseases. After a period of study he helped establish that department at the new medical college where he taught for many years.

Into this active Dallas home with its ever-enlarging horizons, Robert Earl Beddoe was born on September 9, 1882. 721 Exposition Avenue was always home to Robert. It was to this house that his much loved black mare would draw the two-wheeled cart, bringing the sleepy boy home from his paper route. Nearby was a small business district, a shopping center of the early 1900's, where he often made small purchases for the family. While his mother made the buttermilk biscuits for breakfast, Robert would run across to the store to buy steak for four—about ten cents' worth.

It was a busy household, the mother active in church and civic duties, the father a busy doctor and always on call. An orphan girl from the home "lived in" to help with the work, but simple cooking and housework were shared by the children. Robert loved the cooking. And because he so enjoyed good food, he was to become an authority as a gourmet. Students and faculty at Oklahoma Baptist University where he later taught recall his preparation of delightful Chinese cuisine. In later life he enjoyed nothing more than a good dinner with friends at Luchow's in New York.

At certain times Robert handled the telephone for his father, and later briefed him on cases of sickness as they rode on calls around the neighborhood and out in the country by horse and buggy.

In 1882, Dallas was a small muddy town of about 3,000 population, with few paved streets, not yet the fabulous metropolis, the fantastic Big "D" of the next century. The Texas State Fair, established in 1886, was the biggest attraction of the year. It helped create a cosmopolitan atmosphere, as did the artists who often came to Exposition Hall, not far

away from the Beddoe home. Robert took advantage of every
nearby concert and opera. He loved music and was impressed
both by the artists whom he managed to meet and their
performance. Even as a boy, music was a big part of his life.
For the singing at school, at church or for young people's
socials, he was always playing the piano.

Several of the artists who came to Dallas encouraged
Robert to study music. Ed Haury, a representative of the
Pilcher Organ Company, taught him the rudiments of organ
playing as well as the mechanics of the instrument, and
Robert learned to service organs as well as to rebuild them.
Carl Wiseman, a great organist in that day, became his friend
for life.

Robert was encouraged to make music his career. His
evident ability made it a natural choice; his friends and
teachers urged it. This, too, he wanted, but the cost of a
musical education had to be considered. A degree in music
would entail going away to a college or university—there was
no accredited music school in Dallas.

So after graduation from Bryan High School, Robert went
to work—in music.

A cousin of Robert's remembers that the year she lived
with the Beddoes in Dallas to begin her teaching career
(1903–1904), Robert was working with the C. H. Edwards
Music Company. He was also playing the organ for Washington Avenue Church, their family church, and had been for at
least two years. When Washington Avenue Church built a
new building and became Gaston Avenue Church in 1905,
Robert was the new church's first organist, a post which he
held for several years. People still recall his ability and the
thrill it was to listen to him play. And he played the piano
or organ every chance he got, not only for young people's
socials and sing-songs but also for the silent movies.

All this time he was taking advantage of every opportunity
to study music. His cousin recalls that while she was staying

with the Beddoes Robert was taking piano lessons from a fine German professor—"the best in Dallas."

Other influences besides music were at work in Robert's life, however. He grew up under the shadow of, or rather in the climate of, Texas Baptist tradition—a tradition of service and missions. One of his best friends was J. Howard Williams who later became executive secretary of Texas Baptists and the president of Southwestern Baptist Theological Seminary. The Williams and Beddoe families were good friends and neighbors. Dr. Beddoe was the family physician for the Williamses, and the boys, though twelve years apart in age, shared mutual interests of church and school.

As a young boy, Robert accepted Christian principles as they were lived at home—he was devoted to his family and to his church. Under the preaching of that well-known evangelist, Sid Williams, he made his definite decision to be a Christian. He was eleven years old. His grandfather, Dr. Robert Buckner, baptized him. In high school and after graduation he was active in the church (in addition to his organ playing), especially in young people's activities, and with the other young people attended summer assemblies and encampments.

The decision that determined the future course of his life was made at one of these summer meetings. He and a group of church young people had gone to Palacios (Texas) Encampment to hear Dr. George W. Truett preach. In that meeting Robert felt that God was impelling him in a different direction from music. The decision was to make his career, not in music, but in medical missions.

Robert was impressed, of course, by his father's medical career and his active participation in every altruistic enterprise in Dallas. He was also alert to his mother's crusade for missions and her appeals for the unfortunate at home and abroad. And he was inspired by his Uncle Hal's teaching ministry in China. These were potent factors in Robert's decision—yet the decision was his own, his own effort to do something about world needs, to meet the challenges of and to find his identity in the expanding world.

So in 1904 or 1905, with no pre-medical training as we know it today, Robert entered Baylor Medical College in Dallas, the school his father had helped to found.

Baylor! This was part of the rearing of Texas Baptists. But this third generation son of the illustrious line of Baptists who strode into Texas to make history was uniquely different. Pictures of Robert from about this time show a slim, debonair young man with a confident air about him. Able and dedicated, he too was to write history, his in the Far East field of medical missions—another great contribution to the Baptist-Buckner-Beddoe heritage of Texas.

In medical school, Robert's rounds with his father stood him in good stead. So did his music, for Robert also "played his way" through medical training.

Further encouragement for his decision came on a Sunday morning when Dr. J. R. Saunders,[2] representing the Baptist Foreign Mission Board, Richmond, Virginia, spoke to the congregation of Gaston Avenue Church. Dr. Saunders' description of the suffering in the Orient, and the great needs in the fields where Baptists were working, was most impressive, convincing and persuasive. For Robert Beddoe, sitting there near the organ, there was only one word to remember—the need for another doctor in China.

China—that ancient civilization which had survived upheavals and calamities, famines and floods, war and misrule—was of popular interest at that time. People were beginning to know more about China through art and literature and wonderful treasures being brought to our shores. There was, to be sure, adventure to be had in that ageless land of the Far East—but there was also urgent need.

---

[2]Dr. Saunders died early in 1969 in Pacific Palisades, California. He was 95 years old, the oldest living Southern Baptist missionary.

The turn of the century which ushered in the age of enlightenment to America brought turbulence and violence to China. "In 1900, the storm broke. The Boxers, in their characteristic red turbans, broke into the homes of the Chinese Christians and massacred them by the hundreds. Some foreign missionaries were assaulted and murdered. The inventions of the hated foreigners, railway tracks, electric cables, telephone wires, post offices, were torn up, mutilated, or set on fire." [3] The Empress Dowager raged and ordered all Westerners in China put to death. With lovely old Peking mercilessly ravaged and hostilities continuing even after the treaty had been signed, Russia maintained troops in Manchuria, annexing the huge northern provinces, connected to Port Arthur via Trans-Siberian Railroad.

By 1905, the organization Tung Men Hui, with headquarters in Tokyo and with other branches in the United States, France, England, and Germany, rose to the Republican cause. The state was indeed set for revolution, and the flow of Chinese students to America as well as the growing influence of Western-style education in China was to affect decisively the history of their country and seal the fate of dynastic rule.

Slowly, the great wall began to crumble. Western ideas infiltrated the policy of disdainful exclusiveness; modern transportation and communications began to destroy the local isolation; and the cry for reform was heard throughout this vast and remote land. Grover Clark in his book, *The Great Wall Crumbles,* refers to an "external mindedness," an awareness of "international inferiority of China," after believing her race superior for many centuries. Civil wars, agitation, and demonstrations aroused the student population, now organized for revolution and the overthrow of Manchu dynasty which had made Christianity illegal in

[3] Tsui Chi, *A Short History of Chinese Civilization* (New York: G. P. Putnam's Sons, 1943), p. 262.

Robert Earl Beddoe as a medical student

1724. Swift transmission of news up and down the Yangtze Valley hastened developments under the rising Sun Yat-sen, a Hong Kong medical student.

On January 1, 1912, Sun Yat-sen took office, declaring the first day of the first year of the Republic of China. It was also the first day of the third year of Robert Beddoe's mission and ministry to the Chinese people.

3

"The Wrong Girl to Yingtak"

◆—✳—◆

IT WAS indeed a slow boat to China that sailed out of the Golden Gate in late August, 1909. Pacing the deck of the historic old *China,* the twenty-seven-year-old Texas doctor must have been impatient at the many delays of this kind of travel, the endless weeks at sea, the complete isolation from family and home.

There was plenty of time on board, at any rate. There was time for getting acquainted with Miss Annie Sandlin, like him a new recruit going to South China. There was time for preparatory language study and briefing with the Hal F. Buckners, Robert's uncle and aunt who were enroute to Shanghai and later Canton for work in the Baptist Seminary. And there was time to recall the events of the last year, culminating in the bon voyage given the three who would represent Texas in China. Dr. George W. Truett, pastor of the First Baptist Church of Dallas, had expressed the good wishes and high hopes of Texas Baptists and the Foreign Mission Board in his evening sermon that last Sunday, and had commended and encouraged the Buckners and Robert in the dramatic Truett voice and style.

Earlier in the year, on April 29, Robert had graduated from medical school, and his application for service in China had been approved. After an interview with the Board, he was appointed on July 15 to Yingtak in South China, where the Board planned to build a hospital. Also appearing for interviews were two young women who were applying for China. Afterwards it was said that executive secretary J. R. Willingham had assumed the role of Cupid in his appointments, knowing that the Texas doctor was a bachelor. He appointed Miss Annie Sandlin to Yingtak, South China, and Miss Louella Houston to Chefoo in North China. The secretary was quite pleased with his idea and with his selection of a possible bride for the young doctor.

The early missionaries who began the Baptist work in the Yingtak area had erected some buildings for schools, residences, and a church. There had also been some pioneering of medical missions in the area. In North China Dr. John Lake had begun a work among lepers, and Dr. Ayers had started medical work at Hwangshien, Shantung Province.

To the south and west of Yingtak, there had been medical work in Wuchow since 1866 when Dr. R. H. Graves (D.D. and M.D.) began making trips there from Shiu Hing. On his trips he would conduct a dispensary and preach on shore during the day, and live in his boat on the river at night. He was the first missionary of any society to live in the interior of South China, and his medical work drew literally thousands under the influence of the gospel. By 1904 a small hospital building had been built and staffed by Dr. Meadows and Rev. W. H. Tipton, the latter carrying the evangelistic load. But it remained for Dr. Beddoe and his contemporaries to promote a progressive and well-established hospital program in South China in the new century.

Although Robert planned visits to these and other medical programs already in operation, his first energy and time went into serious language study—both the difficult Hakka dialect and Cantonese with its intonations so pleasant to his musical ear. He found his music a real advantage in language study, as well as a friendly grace and a rare comfort in the adjustment to his new world.

During his first years in China, Robert had only temporary housing for a dispensary, with room and equipment for only minor surgery. He made himself available, however, wherever there was need in the village along the river, among officials of the province, among the missionary families of the Baptist compound and of other denominations. He also set about making a new life for himself, enjoying interest in his new friends, new places, new foods, and new developments of Chinese-American relationships. With Yingtak as home base, the young doctor began to explore the surrounding countryside—only an infinitesimal spot in the vast sprawling continent of his pre-voyage map study. China, even without Manchuria, was as large as the U.S. Here lived a fourth of the world's population, and it felt like it. There were people, people everywhere—at every turn within sight and sound.

Eventually Robert became accustomed to this Chinese world so crowded, so crushed. Dallas was nothing like this— streets crowded with rickshas, handcarts, wheelbarrows, coolies balancing baskets on their shoulders, and—as Western influence increased—bicycles. All this in addition to the throngs of people always hurrying. Often the only way to get through a crowd was to elbow yourself along. Along the waterfront of the North River which ran through Yingtak, scores, hundreds of sampans jostled for position, each one the home for families who lived and died on them, sometimes never setting foot on land.

If he was unprepared for the poverty and the disease of the peasant masses, Robert was also apprehensive of the multi-colored comfort of the rich. The contrast was always present—the dirt of the street with the brass, jade, and gorgeous silks which only the rich could afford. The garish,

tinkling decorations on shop fronts, the lanterns and the
bright paper flowers might make you forget the poverty and
disease, but you could never forget the smells of China—the
scent of dried fish; of Oriental herbs and spices and de-
licious foods of all kinds prepared by open-air vendors; the
rotten odors of sewers and refuse dumps exposed to the open
air; the steaming humidity of the market place.

"And whithersoever he entered into villages, or cities, or
country, they laid the sick in the streets, and besought him
that they might touch him, if it were but the border of his
garment" (Mark 6:56).

Diseases of antiquity, all now practically controllable,
raged in the Far East when the young Texas medic set out
on his China mission. "The bubonic plague epidemic with
which all important parts of the world became concerned, is
supposed to have originated in China, in the province of
Yunan, on the Thibetan border, reaching Canton in 1894.
Nearly every country in the world was affected." [1] In 1902,
cholera had spread over India, China, and the Philippines.
As late as 1937–1938, it was still rampant and extremely
severe in China. The refugee influx into certain territories
was an important factor in epidimicity. Cholera made its
appearance in Shanghai every summer from 1889 on, always
with a high mortality rate among the very young and the
very old.

Black fever prevailed from Peking in the north to Canton
in the south, usually in old established villages where vegeta-
tion was allowed to grow up untended. Leprosy was also
prevalent in the low-lying delta of the West River, while
dysentery, typhus, tuberculosis, yellow fever, trachoma, and
the typical ulcerated skin lesions added to the misery of the
masses. Because of malnutrition, anemia and beri-beri af-

---

[1] *Stitt's Diagnosis, Prevention and Treatment of Tropical Diseases*
(Philadelphia: Blakiston Co., 1940).

fected the young for life. Malaria is the world's most infectious disease and has spread the world over by the rapid mobility and transportation of people and goods. In 1939 malaria affected hundreds of thousands of Chinese employed on the China-Burma Highway where supplies of quinine and atabrine were practically unavailable.

Sixty years ago, little was known about the transmission of diseases by insects, rodents, and parasites, nor about the contamination of food and water. It had only been in 1898 that Dr. Ronald Ross had discovered how malaria was carried. Nonexistent sanitary and hygienic measures, native superstitions, and language barriers only added to the prevalence and frequency of disease in this old world into which the young Baylor doctor entered in 1909.

Thirty years later, President Franklin D. Roosevelt, in addressing the National Institute of Health, emphasized that the world had become interrelated and apparently so small that our medical and sanitary responsibilities had greatly increased. "These ramparts we watch must be civilian in addition to military," he said. Stout Memorial Hospital in Wuchow, South China—at this time still in Dr. Beddoe's future—was to become one of these influential ramparts of the Far East.

From the very first, Dr. Beddoe felt that he was inadequate for the ministry of preaching, teaching, and healing he was called to, and that he came to China poorly prepared to execute the directives of the Great Commission. Perhaps every true missionary feels this inadequacy in the face of the need and the poverty of language. This sense drove Dr. Beddoe to supplement his medical knowledge all through his life by graduate work, by interning in new fields of study, and by research into more modern treatments of Oriental diseases. But always, the first priority was the evangelistic message. "Keep up your preaching always," he was to write later to missionary recruits.

Dr. Beddoe's associates in those early days included Dr. Robert E. Chambers of Virginia, the secretary-treasurer of the China Baptist Publication Society. The two Roberts became friends for life and chess partners who often played by correspondence. Other friends were Dr. and Mrs. W. C. Pruitt, who had been his traveling companions on board the *S.S. China* in 1909. They were now stationed in Chefoo up on the Shantung Peninsula, and sent frequent invitations that Robert visit them there.

Then there was that other bachelor from Texas—Fort Worth, that is—Ben Rowland, a missionary evangelist. There was just nobody like Ben, who was to become his closest friend, an American brother. Today, from his California home, Mr. Rowland writes nostalgically of the young Dr. Beddoe, of shared happiness and lonesome times in that Yingtak home on the other side of the world from Fort Worth–Dallas. They were quite a team, these two young bachelors from Texas, and between them, the preaching-healing ministry became increasingly effective.

In North China, another chapter was being added to the Beddoe story. On Christmas Eve, 1909, Miss Louella Houston arrived in Chefoo to begin her missionary career. It would be years before she returned to Kentucky.

The daughter of a Baptist minister, Louella Houston grew up in a family of ten children. After her graduation from Murray High School, she qualified for a teacher's certificate and later attended the Woman's Missionary Union Training School in Louisville for two years. There she met Annie Sandlin, and the two of them became interested in work in China. It was while she was a rural school teacher that she attended a Southern Baptist Convention at Chattanooga, Tennessee, and was impressed by reports of missionary needs.

A link in the chain of missionary interest was her home church and the pastor, Boyce Taylor, who had wanted to spend his life in Brazil but was never able to achieve his goal. Instead, as pastor of a missionary-minded church, he was able to inspire others to go into foreign service and to maintain—against a certain disfavor—a missions-causes-first policy on the home field.

A year as church visitor and evangelistic worker at Troy, Alabama, gave practical experience to this young woman who had set her heart on being a missionary. Summer plans for 1909 included another meeting of the Southern Baptist Convention in Louisville and the long-awaited interview with the Foreign Mission Board in Richmond, Virginia. Among the other aspirants to such a career was the dapper young bachelor, Robert Earl Beddoe.

On board the *S. S. China* late that fall, on its next trip to China, were the newly appointed evangelistic workers, Miss Houston, enroute to Chefoo, North China, and Miss Willie Kelley, missionary-teacher from Alabama, returning from furlough to the Eliza Yates School for Girls, at the North Gate, Shanghai. The voyage was long and difficult, as were most voyages in those days. To this generation, which knows only luxury liners and transworld, jet-propelled air travel, it would have seemed interminable as well as hazardous.

In Chefoo, language study came first. The Mandarin dialect of the North China Mission area came a little hard to Louella, who disclaimed both linguistic and musical aptitudes. The language committee, of which Dr. W. C. Pruitt was chairman, demanded a rigorous class schedule with supplementary teaching under a private tutor. Language study is a part of the discipline and the patient adjustment to service overseas; there can be no communication without an understandable message. Gradually the words came—and communication—and soon friendship.

Throughout the countryside around Chefoo, the young lady from America became a symbol of love and helpfulness, especially for the children. How much there was to do at the mission and among the Chinese Christians in the church! What a blessing to be so busy!

Winter, spring, summer—and the first year in China had passed. Then came the second Christmas. The new spring brought signs of increased interest in Christianity. With slow and difficult Chinese intonations the seed had been sown. There was happiness of heart. It was good to be a missionary.

Now it was Chinese summer. Two interesting passengers were on board a steamer out of Hong Kong to Shanghai and Chefoo: Miss Alice Waters, an educational missionary with the Southern Methodist Women's Board, enroute to a missionary resort home for the summer, and Dr. Robert Beddoe, who had accepted the kind invitation of Dr. and Mrs. Pruitt to be their guest for a few days' visit while on a hospital inspection trip to North China. To honor these summer visitors soon after their arrival in Chefoo, Miss Lottie Moon entertained at dinner in her home at nearby Tungchow. Among the guests was Miss Louella Houston.

"He was so handsome," Louella recalled of Robert Beddoe more than fifty years later, seeing in her mind's eye the dapper figure wearing the white linen suit and the pith helmet with such professional bearing. What a setting for romance and adventure! To meet again, a world away from the conference room of the Foreign Mission Board in Richmond—a familiar face, someone from home, mutual interests and careers. All the prerequisites for happiness seemed to converge on the two young people—who promptly fell in love. The whole missionary compound fell under the spell of their romance.

As vitally important as was the inspection of the medical installations of the North China Mission, it was done as quickly as possible yet with orderly dispatch. The result was a few days of vacation for Robert—time for social evenings with the missionary staff, for strolls along the river, for long serious talks with Louella about their work, their future.

In the summer of 1911, Robert Beddoe left Hong Kong (right) for business and vacation in Chefoo. He traveled by steamer with Miss Alice Waters who was going to visit Miss Louella Houston and they were met by a number of missionaries on the Chefoo pier (above). *From l. to r.:* Dr. W. C. Pruitt, Robert Beddoe, Dr. W. B. Glass, Dr. Newton, Miss Waters, Louella Houston. *Below:* Happy days in Chefoo.

Robert
and Louella
and friends (Mrs.
John Lowe and children)
in Chefoo.

On their
honeymoon
on Dumb-bell
Island.

Prefacing Robert Beddoe's rather formal proposal of marriage was the direct question put in a rather indirect way: "Did you, on coming to China, abandon the thought of home and family while serving as a missionary?" The answer was, of course, "No"—and to the direct question, "Yes"!

So the plans were made. Robert Beddoe and Louella Houston would be married on Louella's birthday, December 9, in Chefoo. It seemed a propitious start to a new life. But plans are made to be changed. As the time approached, the threat of civil war in North China made it necessary to change both time and place of their wedding. It was the year of the Revolution.

"The rising of the students to support the Republican cause in the autumn of 1911 was 'like the blowing of the wind and the gushing of water, like the rolling of thunder,' as a manifesto of the time picturesquely, but with reasonable accuracy, describes it. All up and down the Yangtze Valley, in the far western Szechwan Province, at Canton, and through the South, in the cities, and along the coast, the boys and girls from modernized government and missionary schools swarmed beneath the new five-barred flag of the Republic." [2]

In October, the great revolution broke in earnest and spread beyond the control of the government. Revolutionary forces occupied the heart of China in the center of the Yangtze Valley. From this spark, flames leaped up in all corners of the vast country. Dr. Sun Yat-sen agreed to become temporary president of the Chinese Republic. Greatly beloved by his own circles, he was little known to the masses.

This was China in 1911. What a time to be married, and what a place! In spite of the strife and tension, plans were calmly changed. Every adventure in the rearrangement only added a dramatic touch to the romance.

---

[2] Grover Clark, *The Great Wall Crumbles* (New York: The Macmillan Company, 1935), p. 307.

They were married November 24, 1911, in Shanghai. Rev. Hal Buckner, Robert's uncle, came up to Shanghai from South China to officiate at the ceremony which was held in Miss Willie Kelley's home. Miss Kelley was a witness, as was Mrs. R. T. Bryan who played the wedding march.

After the ceremony, a cablegram was sent to Dr. J. R. Willingham of the Foreign Mission Board—a cablegram still remembered with glee and pride by Louella:

November 24, 1911

You sent the wrong girl to Yingtak, and I am rectifying the mistake.

Robert E. Beddoe, M.D.

4

Home Is Where the Heart Is

—◆❊◆—

"TSO-SHUN, ping-on, Pat Tsai-shi Fu-yan." "Good morning, Christian greetings (peace), Mrs. Robert Beddoe!"

All the Chinese Christians were at the gate of the compound in Yingtak to welcome the new member of the missionary team—Mrs. Robert Beddoe. The chorus of greetings sounding her new Chinese name seemed a fitting introduction to both her new identity and the new chapter of missionary work beginning for Robert and Louella. All her life Louella would remember that welcome at Yingtak.

On the way from Shanghai to South China there had been time for a brief honeymoon in a rented stone cottage on Dumb-bell Island, two hours off the coast. To this missionary resort several families, including the Hal Buckners, had gone to escape the revolutionary fighting now raging in all that area. They all enjoyed companionship in the activities of the oldest Baptist church in China. There was a party in honor of the new bride given by Mrs. Hal Buckner. So for a while the war on the mainland was forgotten.

With a Kentucky bride the young medic was on his way. Talent, education, skill, happiness—all these ingredients to success only renewed his dedication, his determination to overcome every obstacle to being the best missionary doctor possible. He made big plans that would eventually materialize. He found his happiness in his love and in the peace of his home—in bits of color and beauty, in his fondness for Chinese food, in the softly intoned cadences of the Cantonese. Where a piano was available, he would take time to remember and play his favorite pieces of music.

Now he could really settle down to work.

The town of Yingtak is on the North River, one of the three prongs of the Pearl River. It was on the border between the Hakka-speaking and the Cantonese-speaking areas. One approached the city with Big Finger Point Mountain in view behind it, through an open area outside the town where lepers lived in dilapidated buildings, Tall, waving bamboo grew along the banks of the river.

The work of the mission was directed mainly to the Hakka people who were responsive and alert to Christianity. Here the Buckners, Miss Sandlin, Miss Harrison, and Dr. and Mrs. J. R. Saunders were stationed, along with the Beddoes and that Fort Worth bachelor, Ben Rowland. The group became wonderful friends, almost like a family.

When the Hal Buckners were transferred to Canton, to the Seminary there, Robert and Louella Beddoe moved into their home, a two-story gray brick building, with living room, dining room, study, and kitchen on the first floor, and bedrooms on the second. Wide verandas around the house were designed for air cooling. Ben Rowland became a member of the family, although later he, too, substantiated the theory that a bachelor missionary "lasts only three years" and was married to Miss Pearl Harrison of the missionary staff. (Dr. William Wallace was a later exception to this theory.)

There were two hospitals in Yingtak, German and English; another was needed. Could Southern Baptists afford it— at this time? The answer came in a gift from the States, a modest sum to be sure, but enough to begin. On the west bank of the North River, below Yingtak, a small hospital was soon under construction. As an interesting innovation, split bamboo was used instead of steel reinforcement for the concrete, proving to be both satisfactory and inexpensive. This was a practical, functional building, constructed by local carpenters and masons under the supervision of the young doctor who had watched builders back in Dallas change the face of that city—and remembered what he had seen.

There were happy, busy days as the Beddoes began their life together on the missionary compound. Louella began to listen carefully to the new sounds of the Cantonese dialect, trying to attune her ear to the more varied "ups and downs" of communication than she was accustomed to hearing. Indeed, this change in dialect had been a serious consideration affecting her acceptance of Dr. Beddoe's proposal. As hard as Mandarin had been, Cantonese seemed even more difficult, with its eight different tones to Mandarin's four. Private teachers came to the rescue, especially old Shu Sien-shang (Teacher Shu), remembered for his patient, careful coaching. Gradually there was communication between the new bride and her teachers, the servants, the Chinese Christian friends. She began to be understood at the church and in the clinic. Her Lop-Tsop (miscellaneous) classes with children marked the beginning of her evangelistic work in the South China Mission.

The Beddoe home became the center of activity for both church and community and a guest house for all visitors, new missionaries, and those enroute to other stations. As the wife of a busy doctor, she managed an important household. Even with servants, housekeeping duties were numerous; there were no time-saving gadgets, no conveniences, no refrigeration. Staple food supplies were brought by boat from Hong Kong, a two-day trip. Sawdust-lined tin boxes would keep things "cool" for quite a while, but not in very hot weather.

Once, during a severe heat wave, Dr. Beddoe's block of ice, ordered through the steward on the boat, melted so rapidly that there was only enough ice left for one pitcher of water— such a luxury on a hot humid day.

In the first home there were two servants, Ah Kun and his wife Ah Sho, without whom the Beddoes could not have carried on their many mission duties. Their little seven-year-old son used to work and play in the courtyard with a baby girl strapped to his back. According to custom, she had been bought cheaply at an early age to become his wife when they both grew a little older.

With the progress of the new hospital, the reputation of the clinic grew among the Chinese. The days were never long enough to see all who came for treatment. Dr. Liang was one of the first to be associated with Dr. Beddoe. A third-generation Christian, the fruit of Presbyterian missions, he was an able physician. How impressed he was, how deeply touched, when his name appeared one time on a Southern Baptist prayer calendar along with the Beddoes' names, and he realized he was prayed for by all Southern Baptist women.

Mei Sun—Mary Frances—came to be a Christmas present to the Beddoes on December 22, 1912. "Beautiful" and "new" were the Chinese words for her name, chosen by Shu Sien-shang in honor of relations between America and a new China. The American baby, born in Matilda Hospital on the Peak in Hong Kong, seemed symbolic of better relations between the two republics. Before she was a year old, her great-grandfather, Robert Buckner of Dallas, had traveled around the world in 1913 to welcome her to the family.

Addie Buckner Beddoe, named for her paternal grandmother, joined the family on August 1, 1914. Mei Yuk, Beautiful Pearl, was her Chinese name. The two girls grew up to speak Cantonese, to play with Chinese playmates, and to take part in all the children's activities of the mission compound. Their early grade education was under their

Dr. Robert Buckner traveled around the world to visit his grandson, Robert Beddoe, and his great-granddaughter in Yingtak.

Below: Robert Beddoe holds Mary Frances.

Scenes of old China. Men and mules were two means of transportation—and always with a well-balanced load.

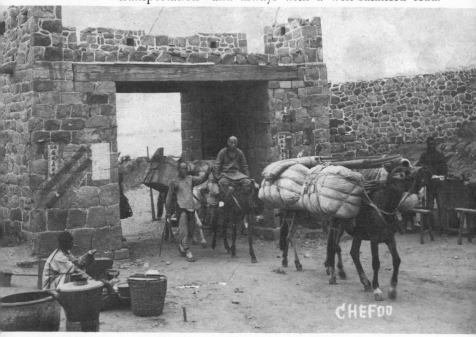

mother's part-time direction. Later they attended British schools. When they eventually came to America for public school education, their English seemed strange to American children, and they found idiomatic "American" another language to be learned.

Each spring brought serious flooding along the North, East, and West Rivers, often inundating the whole country as well as the mission compound. Relief work, directed by the Red Cross, became a part of the doctor's duties, along with providing what medical care he could. Rice was distributed by the missionaries with the help of Standard Oil lighters and Chinese gunboats, as well as medicines and what other foods were available. Through every such emergency, the young doctor proved himself capable and calm, and his administrative leadership increased. In these practical ways Christian love and concern was shown.

Robert Beddoe saw his ministry as one of "go-preach-teach-heal." The thinking he did on the purpose and strategy of missions at this time later became the basis for orientation courses which he felt should be required of every missionary appointee. He was aware of the barriers of language and culture, of the ancient tradition and philosophy of Chinese scholars, as well as the variance of Eastern and Western attitudes. He believed in learning Chinese well, both language and culture. He also sensed the Chinese attitude of responsibility, and believed in honoring it by placing Chinese in positions of leadership. An important factor in missionary work, he felt, was an effective liaison between governments in all the complex relationships of today's knowledgeable world.

In line with his view that he was a missionary first, Dr. Beddoe arranged to take several boat trips with Dr. Saunders to various out-stations while the new hospital was being constructed. It was generally customary for the missionaries to take along some American food on these trips—a tin of melba toast, some cans of milk or other items that would keep indefinitely. But Robert Beddoe relished Chinese cooking and accepted every invitation to eat with Chinese Christians.

There were always delays on these trips. Sometimes they were hours late getting to meetings. Sometimes they were guided to the place of meeting at night by a dim light and the singing of hymns by those who waited in the darkness. As Robert thought back on these experiences, they became symbolic of his mission in China.

Politically in China, the situation had not improved. Strife and insecurity continued in the wake of civil wars. Sun Yat-sen, temporary president of the Republic, realized that if the revolution were to succeed, he must reach some agreement with his opponent, Yuan Shih-k'ai, an ambitious politician and head of a powerful army. He therefore offered him the presidency if he would support the revolution. "Deserted by their most powerful and able statesman, the Emperor and his supporters realized that their hour had come. The Emperor abdicated; the Republic was given birth; the country belonged to the people!" [1]

By 1913, however, tension rose between Yuan and Dr. Sun, and a coalition of war lords invited Yuan to mount the throne. But when rebellion broke out in the South, Yuan's courage began to ebb, and the enthronement was postponed. "From Yuan's death in 1916 till the second revolution in 1926, China was at the mercy of contending rulers . . . their public administration was as worthless as their personal behavior. Education was entirely neglected; industry, so sorely needed by the country, was discouraged. Most of the schoolmasters and employees in public utility services remained unpaid. . . . The war lords were immeasurably rich." [2]

[1] Tsui Chi, *op. cit.*, p. 278.
[2] *Ibid.*, p. 279.

It seemed a bad time to go home to take a furlough. China in 1915, so beset with internal problems, needed the doctor now. And not only was there a war in China, but there was war in Europe, with the United States slowly becoming involved. However, there came an offer of a surgical internship at Baylor University. So to 721 Exposition Avenue (the upstairs of the family home made into an apartment) in Dallas, Robert Beddoe returned. There was only a trace of the dashing debonair now. The adventure of the youth had become a serious responsibility of the man, the doctor—to heal, to teach, to preach to a needy world. And he had a wife and daughters to care for.

Home meant family gatherings, paved streets, cars, good fitting clothes, Texas food, music and concerts, and beautiful services at Gaston Avenue Baptist Church. There were Sunday afternoon organ-piano concerts in the chapel of Buckner Orphan's Home; Carl Wiseman, who was then president of the National Guild of Organists, and Robert Beddoe would perform for all the children and their guests. Often the two would exchange parts and instruments.

Most of all, being home meant an opportunity to tell "his story" upon every invitation. It also meant study and surgical knowledge directed toward China.

Complete personal fulfillment for the Beddoes came in the birth of a son, Robert Stanley, on February 17, 1917, in Texas. In their happiness, the Beddoes could almost forget the plight of China, or the war in Europe.

But not quite. War soon touched the United States. Although news from foreign lands reached Texas slowly, and in rural areas the newspapers were always a day or two late, still in every American home, where neighbors came "to sit until bedtime," children heard the horrors of war talk. Big headlines announced the sinking of the *Lusitania*. And eventually the winter-muddy trenches of the French front were filled with American doughboys. On every Main Street across the country there was parading, flag-waving patriotism, while red crosses on Volunteer Nurses' uniforms could hardly keep up with the gold stars in the windows.

In spite of the war, it was a time of great expansion for Baptists, an era of school building, both colleges and seminaries, and of the beginning of an ambitious hospital program. Construction started on a Baptist hospital in Dallas to affiliate with Baylor Medical School. The Baptist Memorial Hospital in Houston was hailed as the "greatest thing that has happened to this part of Texas." There was plenty to do for an ambitious young Baptist doctor in Texas.

But not for Robert Beddoe.

5

Halfway Around in 40 Days

DALLAS—El Paso—San Francisco—Honolulu—Yokohama—Kobe—Shanghai—Hong Kong—Canton—Yingtak. This was the Beddoe itinerary on their return to China in 1918.

March 15, 1918, ten days from San Francisco, three days from Honolulu: "Now that the leave-taking is all over and we have begun to face the next seven years in China, I look forward with deep pleasure to the return. I have begun to remember friend after friend and to long to see them, many among the missionaries, many fine Chinese friends to see. Yes, I am really anxious to get back. The vexing question as to whether or not we should move to Wuchow, I am not going to permit to vex me. As soon after reaching Yingtak as possible, I want to arrange a long country trip to visit the Hakka churches. I want to take helpers and medicine and a preacher. I want to get my language back, and this is the best way to do so. Moreover, I wish to see firsthand the exact conditions along the first-line trenches. I can hardly wait for this time to come. . . ."

The diary, called *Moving Thoughts,* begun in San Francisco on a Sunday morning, March 3, 1918, became a sizable book and could have been a best seller on today's market. It describes a trip over halfway around the world with the Beddoes and their children—Mary Frances, Addie B., and Robert Stanley—traveling with the Hal Buckners and their children—Robert Cooke, Jo, Franklin, and Travis.

After an exhausting train trip over Texas plains and desert country, a few hours' layover at the hotel in El Paso afforded baths all around and time to buy some fresh food and some powdered milk for the baby. The lunch supply prepared by the home folks was all gone now. Because the family would want to know, Dr. Beddoe carefully and patiently described every detail of the care of the fretful children across the endless miles to San Francisco. Here, the few days to prepare for the voyage were used up in the formalities of departure, the red tape of tickets, passports, and baggage inspections. Then there was the interview with the British Consul to request passage through Hong Kong. Accumulated mail had to be answered. Telegrams had to be sent. Canned food and milk had to be packed, and some fresh fruit bought to carry on board.

The last state-side Sunday was described as ". . . an eventful day . . . all our days are so far for that matter. The vexing question of food for Mary Frances and Addie B. takes up about four hours . . . . I had breakfast at a little joint on Market Street where I got a lovely thick loin steak, fried onions, potatoes, and coffee for thirty cents. In the middle of the morning, I walked out with Uncle Hal and we went to the Chinese Baptist Church, but it was too early and we were unable to get hold of anyone. I was anxious to see the pastor for I knew him quite well in China. When we got back, I took charge of Robert Stanley, and Louella and the girls started to church. I had just gotten the bottle fixed and managed to write a few lines of this letter when they came back, having failed to get to church because of poor car service—so we miss our Dodge very much. About two-thirty p.m., I started out with Uncle Hal to the organ recital by the famous Edwin H. Lemare. The wonderful Exposition organ, presented to the city by the Exposition, is installed in the auditorium. It was very fine, and I enjoyed every minute of the hour."

When would he ever hear such music again?

With no shortcuts to travel, no quick disposition of details, the two families and their assorted baggage of sixteen trunks, nine suitcases, and innumerable bundles and boxes were assembled on the dock. The old *China,* the familiar ship now forty years old and showing it, waited to take on the eighty tons per day coal supply required to Honolulu. Bon voyage greetings and letters from friends, one to be opened every day of the voyage, did little to assuage the ache that came when the "last tie was severed," for after once boarding the ship, no one was permitted to go ashore again.

"There isn't anything in this town but water," Addie B. said that first day out when four-year-old excitement began to wear. "And isn't this a rocky, old boat?" was Mary Frances' six-year-old comment. And then, seasickness. Only those who have experienced such indescribable malaise can imagine the plight of a distraught father, still on his feet but bone-tired, in his ministrations to his family. He himself was never seasick.

"We are now forty-eight hours out of San Francisco, and Louella has had only one glass of malted milk since her breakfast at the hotel two days ago. She tried to help with the baby's bottle, etc., but she has been unable to do a thing since except to watch him for a short time while I eat. . . .

"At present my schedule is anything but interesting. The children have to eat at seven, twelve, and six. My meals are due at eight, one, and seven. Robert Stanley is due to eat at six, ten, two, six, and ten. He has a short nap in the morning, in the afternoon, and sleeps at night until about four in the morning when my day begins. It is a man's job to take care

of him, not to mention all the other things, washing his
bottles, trying to get milk, trying to get his barley flour
cooked, etc. . . . Miss Blanche Rose Walker (missionary),
an angel of light, is on board. She came to the cabin a while
ago to help and to comb Louella's hair—just in time to keep
me from jumping overboard. . . ."

Moments stolen from baby-watching found the doctor at
his Corona typewriter, his fingers pounding to record the
days for the family at home and to philosophize on life in
general. This was his escape, his therapy for frustration,
disappointment, distress and happiness. Out of all this would
come a plan of action, a program-directive for the next seven
years in China. He was a fine writer and journalist, a detail
man, logician, who wrote everything down, as though to
clear his brain, to reassert his ideas on the missionary concept. It was, too, a reaffirmation of his personal dedication to
God's compelling purpose.

In those few times of solitude, on the deck of the old
China, he shared his intimate thoughts, his dedicated spirit,
his unique grace with the folks in Murray, Kentucky, and
Dallas, Texas. He tried to prepare them—and himself—for
what lay ahead.

In moments of fatigue and depression, he remembered the
happy exhilaration of the farewell service in Dallas. Again,
Dr. Truett had launched the party. Off Honolulu, completely cut off from world news, he wrote: "Of course, we are
anxious for news. We hope that if the 'Sammies' do any
stunts, we will hear of it. They are going to do some stunts
all right, when the proper time comes. I am sure you all
know my attitude in this matter. If the time comes that I
am needed and Uncle Sam wants to find me, he will not have
to hunt for me; and when he does find me, I will be on my
way to meet him."

He and Uncle Hal talked all this over as they waited for
some word on the American-Allied advance in Europe and

as they tried to manage writing time. Their little running
feud on "reporting" broke the monotony of the long voyage,
each trying to out-write the other in keeping notes, writing
letters, addresses, and sermons. Uncle Hal was often ahead—
but his children were older! And that made a difference!

On Sundays, Mr. Buckner preached for the church service,
and Dr. Beddoe accompanied the singing. The congregation,
however, was mainly the missionary personnel of many denominations traveling to distant posts. Sensitive to injustice
and criticism, to humiliating abuse and ridicule, Dr. Beddoe
deeply resented discriminating remarks by other passengers
about "those missionaries" and never failed to assert himself
and his qualifications for service abroad. He resented, too,
having to travel on this old boat, so grimy from forty years
of hard use.

With all the discomfort and inconvenience, these were
days of loving and studying the children, each with his own
identity, every reaction to certain situations recorded by a
devoted and proud father. "Six-year-old Addie B. is still
worrying about leaving all her friends (in Dallas). She said
the other day she wished she did not know about China so
she would not have to go. She asked me if I would go if she
did not, and I told her, 'No.' 'Well, if I just didn't know
about China, I wouldn't go and then you wouldn't know, but
I do know about it so we must go.' " He reported Mary
Frances' bad dreams, her fear of the boat's turning over—
these fears, illnesses, and discomforts had to be handled by
anxious parents. And everything was so strange for the baby.

Plans for Honolulu and a much-needed rest for the grown-
ups, as well as for the children, were ruined by rain, as were
the Kodak pictures they had wanted. The long-anticipated
day at the beach and the streetcar ride from the dock were
only a disappointed dream. All too soon, the five o'clock boat
whistle started the family on their way again.

"Six more days before we reach Yokohama, then the rush

and irregularity connected with entering and leaving port, then two more Japanese ports, then Shanghai, and then Hong Kong. We are all tired of the boat . . . now we are about to enter the Hell-Hole of Japan, the part of the Pacific which is most dreaded by mariners because it is so often storm swept. It is also the deepest water in the world, being over five miles deep. . . ."

How the children enjoyed Yokohama where three rickshas were needed to give them a bit of sightseeing! Bundled up because of the severe cold, they were excited about this storybook adventure among the friendly, courteous Japanese people who stood to watch these strange visitors from America. Off Kobe, a furious typhoon threatened the creaking, old vessel. Robert described in detail these anxious hours. ". . . if, under all the circumstances, God was pleased to take us all home at once, I was perfectly willing and ready. I had not the slightest doubt that anything of the sort would happen, for I firmly believe that He has His work for us to do in China." Ashore briefly at Nagasaki, as the storm subsided, the two families made enthusiastic plans to return to Japan some day for a vacation.

In Shanghai, inflation became apparent when the men exchanged their U.S. gold for Mexican silver. "We have to buy everything out here with Mexican money, and it may become really serious. True, the Board has promised to give us two for one; but with war conditions at home and the price of Mexican silver reaching the sky, I seriously doubt that the Board will be able to support us. It will be hard on the Board and hard on the missionaries; but when good news comes from France, as it most certainly will someday, the exchange rate will be more favorable."

The typewriter keys were still clicking toward the last port call. The nearer the ship to Hong Kong, the more anxious Dr. Beddoe was to see the friends at the mission station, especially Ben Rowland, his pal, "one of the finest men I ever knew, a man of fine judgment, of religion and zeal—not puritanical." The only disagreement ever in their friendship was over the relative sizes of Ft. Worth and Dallas in 1918—"I will be *awful* glad to see old Ben again."

Encouraging reports were verified upon arrival; Ben was careful about examining candidates for baptism and had done fine foundation work, both in the church and in the boys' school. The atmosphere in Yingtak was far more favorable than it had been, and the work of the mission was beginning to be respected—"a new thing and a condition which I did not have faith to report for many years . . . the evangelistic and educational work are most hopeful, and all bearing on the medical." The work of Ben and his wife, the former Pearl Harrison, among the Hakka people was remarkable and noteworthy.

"Another kindred spirit is Dr. Leavell at Wuchow, one with whom I can talk matters over in complete understanding, a Southerner, and that probably explains the main reason why I am attracted to him. In the event I should move to Wuchow, I feel very sure we would get along beautifully." His thoughts raced ahead—much faster than the ship steaming nearer the coast line. April 2, 1918—10 A.M.—"We will soon be there."

The civil war in China had been going on six months when the Beddoes arrived in Yingtak, May 4, 1918. A month later, Dr. Beddoe was called to Shin Quan to take charge of a military base hospital. Several of the Southern provinces had formed a separate government, which resulted in fighting among the factions, the Southerners representing the more democratic party. The wounded arrived steadily from up-river skirmishes. Louella and the children, however, were safe in Yingtak, in no danger, Dr. Beddoe felt, for the fighting had to come through Shin Quan before it could reach them.

Reporting on an early spring revival there, Dr. Beddoe

spoke of much interest in the church—"50 decisions," many of whom were soldiers temporarily located there. "It was a fine meeting and indicated that the Chinese are far more anxious to listen to solid preaching than to hear arguing against idols. Good crowds came for every service, the new converts accepting responsibility for the others."

While at Shin Quan, he lived, ate, slept, talked, and thought Chinese. To have brought a cook, with all the supplies and utensils necessary for the preparation of American food, would have been difficult and impractical. Fortunately, he was well-satisfied with Chinese food. As to a bed, that was something else! Impossible to bring his own, he learned to sleep Chinese fashion—on flat boards placed across two work benches with a piece of matting and a cotton pad about one inch thick; a pillow, his one concession to comfort, substituted for the Chinese block of wood.

War and slaughter continued, atrocities too horrible to mention. At one time every patient in a mission hospital was killed by entering soldiers. All prisoners of war were promptly executed. "When will the world have peace?" was the anguished cry of the Texas doctor on the front lines in the Far East.

"At the time when the young Chinese Republic struggled to birth, the foreign powers had nicely adjusted their 'spheres of influence' in China and were at pains to see that no one of them enjoyed greater rights or larger territorial concessions than the rest. But with the outbreak of the European War of 1914-1918, this balance of power was shaken to pieces. Germany, Russia, Great Britain, France, and Belgium were all too deeply involved in their own deadly struggle to safeguard their interests in China, while Japan, the villain of Asia, was free to seize her golden opportunity and to assert her long desired domination of the Far East by every means, fair or foul, that lay in her power." [1] Manchuria was

---

[1]Tsui Chi, *op. cit.,* p. 285.

her goal, her demands were asserted on the famous white papers.

At the outset of the European war, China decided to remain neutral, ineffectively protesting that Japan had extended her operations beyond the former German territory. There followed, on the part of the Chinese people, disillusionment and disgust at a series of injustices, indignations, and evidences of government dishonesty. All this stirred the student movements and, thus, the whole nation. The educated class, having been guided through the writings of Confucius, began to realize that they had been living in a classical dream of the past. "New times produce their own prophets. Confucius had lived some five hundred years before Christ when China was already 'civilized,' when modern Europe had not even been born and America was an undiscovered continent. Now, after more than two thousand years, the Western powers had shown only too clearly their lordship over the earth while China appeared to be passing into an abyss of stagnation. Some fundamental change seemed imperative." [2]

Along with the political movement, there developed among the students that great cultural renaissance of modern China, the New Civilization movement. It was a time for the young, the beginning of education for women and of their participation in national life. The new movement in literature, however, brought many young people into the Communist Party, its novel basic principles appealing to many. The Communists, in the meantime, had been experimenting in social reforms in the territory under their control.

And so much had happened at Yingtak in the short years of furlough. There was the smell of revolution and war in the air. Evangelistic emphasis was more important now than ever. It seemed years since Dr. Beddoe had written in his diary: "Dr. Phon, who took charge of the hospital in Yingtak

[2]*Ibid.*, p. 287.

when I left, will be valuable help to me in my work. His presence in Yingtak will permit me to do some medical itineration I have always wanted to do. I will be able to leave Yingtak for weeks at a time and feel reasonably safe about my family and work. About his person, he is inclined to be a bit careless; perhaps this gives him a better hold upon the common run of Chinese. I may, later on, overcome this fault of his by requiring all hospital employees to wear a uniform. He reminds me of an old-fashioned family country doctor, and he knows more about treating Chinese ailments than I do."

As he wrote, he planned—with five suggestions taken from his notes—for evangelistic emphasis.

1. As many hospital women and preachers as there are medical staff.

2. A room for an evangelistic center.

3. The extension work: Bibles and Christian literature, medical supplies.

4. Many "heard the gospel first at the hospital."

5. The work of the Christian Mission Alliance Associational Missionary must be emphasized.

Typical of the evangelistic crusades in Yingtak were preparations and announcements similar to contemporary procedures in our churches fifty years later. Each day the sermon would be illustrated on a large blackboard placed by the roadside, near the entrance of the church. About an hour before each service, several bands of 'workers' went into the homes and along the streets inviting the people, particularly the children, to come to the service. Mrs. Beddoe and the girls went about quietly; the boys, although accompanied by their elders, were not so quiet but were effective in their advertising. It was a time for parades and bright banners.

Things were not always serious in the Beddoe household or even on the mission compound. There were many happy family times when the girls were not in school—Louella taught them by the Calvert System—and Robert wasn't busy. Robert Beddoe had a sense of fun and a delightful sense of humor. In a light-hearted moment he wrote this poem for his family in Yingtak.

On the Banks of Old North River

On the banks of the old North River
There's a city named *Yingtak.*
If you've not heard its history, ever,
You have surely missed a lot.
Here's the home of all the Beddoes;
And our Ku Ngiong, "San y" true;
And the new and loved Bethamen—
We're a jolly, happy crew.

There is "Thai Tsi"; "Little Sister";
Robert Stanley and A Shiu;
There is "Robbie" and "Louella";
"Ben" and "Perle" and Yong A Mu.
There's A Ngi, A Kiau and Sin Fwei;
Of the teachers there're a lot;
And I tell you, we are *happy,*
At our compound in *Yingtak.*

Still our life is filled with sadness
By the pests that here abound;
And our bodies itch with madness,
As they compass us around.
Gnats, flies and mosquitoes,
And white ants by the ton!
While the fleas conspire to eat us,
E'er our work on Earth is done.

But our Church and Schools, progressing,
And the Book Room, spreading light;
And the Master's every blessing,
Makes our life and labors bright.
Here our Sunday School and Union
Have an active Normal Class,

Where the workers, in communion,
Are bringing things to pass.

With the mountains all around us;
And the Finger Point, so bold;
With the birds and flowers about us—
These're our blessings manifold.
For the love which binds together
Our hearts in service true;
Is the thing, that, in all weather,
Makes us glad the whole year through.

"The vexing problem" which boarded the ship with the family in March, 1918, had now to be resolved. So in 1919 Dr. Beddoe and his family moved to Kwangsi Province and to the staff of Stout Memorial Hospital. There Robert Beddoe began the larger part of his work in China. He was preceded in Wuchow by the impressive Dr. George W. Leavell of the well-known Southern Leavells, whose heritage, like that of the Buckner-Beddoe family, lives on in succeeding generations. As able doctor and administrator, Dr. Leavell had developed an outstanding medical missions program in the somewhat modest first building of Stout Memorial opened in 1904. Dr. Beddoe was able to add additional floors to the original structure and to extend wings, terraces, and living facilities for nurses and staff. Raising money for such extensive construction was his first responsibility. Eventually, Stout Memorial became one of the Southern Baptists' most impressive institutions. During normal times, it was self-supporting, even with all the charity work at the clinic.

With the banner line, "Evangelize, Baptize, Indoctrinate," four thousand copies of the 1919 Report of Stout Memorial Hospital were distributed over the Southern Baptist Convention that year. A fine journalist, Dr. Beddoe made the most of the printed word to stimulate interest and to dramatize the mission enterprises in foreign lands. The effect of the missionary sermon, he felt, was all too often lost in the superficial and belittling sympathy inspired by tales of hardships and sacrifice. To counteract this with the constituency, he wrote with careful logic and precise phrasing, usually typing his own correspondence, lectures, and reports.

The 1919 report indicated advance in every department of the hospital, a steady and healthy growth. Most remarkable was the work in the Free Clinic Department where Mrs. Beddoe spent each day with Bible women and the Christian women of the Wuchow Church, "talking the gospel to individual women patients and keeping them quiet during the Chaplain's daily sermon." Advances in evangelistic work at the boys' school were also reported by Dr. Beddoe, who assumed responsibilities there for a time in addition to that of the hospital administration. Colportage work, a most challenging venture, resulted in a "True Light Book Room" in Wuchow, a clearing house for all Colportage, and the ordering and transshipping of Bibles and tracts. The Baptist ladies of Kentucky voted to provide the hospital with bandages and gauze for that year. For this, the Beddoes expressed sincere gratitude.

Sociable and outgoing, the Texas doctor set out to win his way in Wuchow, to establish friendly relations with the city and provincial authorities, and to enhance feelings of good will toward the hospital. He was a popular member of the Wuchow Rotary Club. There he came in contact with business and professional men, bankers, government officials. A young Chinese representative of Texaco was a touch of home. A prominent Baptist layman, Lam Chi-fung, was ever the gracious friend and host to the Beddoe family. He was always helpful when it came to shipping hospital supplies from Hong Kong to Wuchow by West River steamers. And the young generalissimo, Chiang Kai-shek, came to inspect the hospital.

Few triumphs are unalloyed. And so it was to be with the

fulfillment of the hospital dream. Out of the actual construction of the hospital came the accidental death of little Robert Stanley, whose three, not quite four, years spanned the Pacific to join two continents. He had wandered under some loose timbers used in the pouring of the concrete which fell and crushed him. In spite of the desperate efforts of the hospital staff, the loving sympathy of missionary and Chinese friends, a page of deep personal tragedy had to be written.

Robert Stanley's boyishness still shines through a picture of him and his daddy singing at the piano, though his "little brother" days are recalled only occasionally by the two big sisters. But then he was deeply missed; his flashes of American charm had brightened the whole mission compound and he was the special delight of his Chinese amah.

Out of this experience came an unusual statement, so far unpublished—a pledge to renewed dedication to God and His work in China:

Wuchow, November 2, 1920

Many years ago we dedicated our lives to China and the Chinese, and for eleven years we have tried, under God, to serve them. We have made many mistakes, for we are but sinners saved by grace; but we have honestly tried to do our best to the end that the comfort of salvation through Christ be brought to Chinese hearts. Now God, in his fathomless wisdom, has brought this great sorrow to our hearts, which instead of turning us from our purpose, shall only serve to increase our zeal and efforts to serve the people of China— our adopted country. We can no longer in truth be called foreigners for now the bone of our bone and flesh of our flesh is mingled with the dust of this land. To our gracious Lord and to those who love his appearing, we renew our pledge for service to the limit of what strength may be given us.

Robert E. Beddoe
Louella H. Beddoe

"As the mountains are round about Jerusalem," so are mountains around about Wuchow. And all these years, the little grave on a hillside overlooking Wuchow has been a tribute to Christian courage. Nearby is the memory of another stalwart, Dr. William L. Wallace, a big, tall man who would want to comfort a little boy. "And if he cries, the angels will rock him"—there in the shade of the green bamboo.[3]

---

[3]From a poem written by Albert F. Beddoe.

6

A Marginal Note—II Cor. 4:8

MOTHERS remember everything, cherishing precious memories not for telling. The ache remains, but it, too, is one's own. A dauntless spirit shone through the greatest tragedy a mother can bear, the loss of a child. As is every child, Robert Stanley was so special. The chubby little boy who grew tired and fretful on that long, tiresome voyage, fulfilled his own brief destiny. He was the little Texan of the family.

"But not in despair"—these brave words, written as a marginal note in Louella's Bible to II Corinthians 4:8, reveal the fortitude of both mother and father. Louella Beddoe recalls how she and Robert remade their plans to vitalize those shipboard dreams of a more intensive evangelistic effort, with medical and evangelistic teams going by river boat to remote out-stations. If Dr. Beddoe or some other staff member were unable to leave the hospital, a male nurse would go with the local pastor or a Bible woman. The hospital proved an ideal base of operations for the preaching, teaching, healing ministry of a generation ago.

In those days it was a composite career. Later it evolved

into a "specialist" concept, one person a specialist in medicine, another in evangelism or teaching. In our time there seems to be a return to the earlier concept of the wholeness of foreign mission ministry. This is seen in the activation of the Peace Corps and the VISTA program. The policy of apprenticeship by associate missionaries, recently instituted by the Southern Baptist Foreign Mission Board as well as many other boards, affirms the importance of living and being on the mission field. The whole person is important, not just his words. A return to this concept can help the slowed-down process of world evangelization to regain its momentum.

Somehow at Wuchow the months went by. The concrete was poured; the mixing troughs were hauled away. The hospital, with modern construction of brick and reinforced concrete and cement-tiled floors was splendidly magnificent in its day. The interiors of the first floor and most of the second floor had been finished in 1919. Dr. Beddoe had written about it: "The beautiful operating room on the second floor will compare favorably with the operating rooms of our most modern hospitals anywhere in America. Ample in size, well-lighted, with floors and wainscoting paved with snow-white porcelain tiles, it is beautiful indeed. Adjoining facilities include a room for various sterilizers, another room for surgical supplies, and a washroom for the surgeons."

There was, however, one urgent need to be met. This fine facility, staffed by skillful doctors operating in glistening white rooms, had only one small X-ray, which was usable only for bone work. There was only one other machine in all of Kwangsi Province for more than eight million people, but it was inaccessible and impractical for most cases. While home on furlough, Dr. Leavell presented this emergency to the Foreign Mission Board who appropriated $1,500.00 in three shipments for additional operating sterilizing equipment and later a modern X-ray machine. Stout Memorial Hospital was ready for expanded service.

Soon after the dedication of the new building at Stout Memorial, Dr. Leavell and his family left Wuchow for furlough. As a result, the responsibility of the hospital and the many involvements of management fell on the shoulders of Dr. Beddoe. Describing the awesome task, Dr. Beddoe wrote: "It was a straining of the heart strings to see the Wuchow– Hong Kong steamer slowly turn Eastward and gather speed as the forms and faces and waving handkerchiefs of our dear friends grew indistinct in the distance. It was a call to closer cooperation with God, a time for re-consecration, re-commission, and renewed realization of the futility of trusting in human strength and wisdom."

Robert felt it imperative to continue organizational plans perfected by Dr. Leavell, carrying out in the minutest detail every directive and policy in the management of this large enterprise. In addition to a full schedule of surgery and clinical supervision, it was necessary to make note of every business procedure, to check daily supplies of food and maintenance, to create a disciplinary atmosphere for nurses and staff, and to handle intricate diplomatic relations of U.S.– Chinese liaison. Mr. Chan, proficient in business and accounting, was invaluable help in such matters. The financial statement of 1919 reported treatment for 38,033 patients with total receipts of $12,546.17. Expenditures reached $12,439.30, with a balance on hand of $106.87.

Later, Stout Memorial Hospital was given the contract for medical care of University students. "After weeks of tactful negotiations," Robert wrote home, "I obtained a contract to have the medical supervision of the students of the great government school, Kwangsi University, for the ensuing scholastic year. Besides helping us financially, this will give us contact with over one thousand students and will considerably bolster our standing in the community. . . . The Stout Memorial Hospital (Wuchow) has always held free clinics for the people every day except Sunday—and many

Rex Ray,
Robert Beddoe,
and
Sun Yat-sen
in 1921.

Dr. and Mrs. Beddoe with the medical and evangelistic hospital staff.   *Foreign Mission Board photo.*

Chinese Christians can say 'I heard the Gospel first at Stout Memorial Hospital.' " The hospital drew patients from many parts of the Province, sustaining a program of extension to reach out for those "other sheep" by the wayside. Thousands of pages of literature were distributed, the expenses of this met out of current hospital receipts and mission money.

A nursing program under the supervision of Miss Winnie Kong was most effective in the training of young Chinese girls in this urgent field. Later, Miss Kong married the brilliant Dr. Leung On-fuk, a third-generation Christian, who was on the staff of the Hospital. Dr. Leung, after studying with Dr. Hayes, became invaluable to the work of the dispensary and hospital in the treatment of eye, ear, nose, and throat diseases. Although he was the son of a Wesleyan Methodist pastor, he was later baptized into the Baptist Church. Dr. Go Kin-hing, a successful woman doctor, interned here, serving ten years on the medical staff before going into private practice. Another well-known staff doctor was Dr. Wang Min-chi. He and the others were effectual workers in the local church.

By 1922, the missionary compound in Wuchow, though never completely adequate, was an impressive sight. From the clinic on the street level, broad concrete steps approached the main building of the hospital, now five stories high. Many trans-world visitors were entertained in the doctor's home nearby. They remembered the hospitality afforded by the spacious airiness in a tropical setting, whether in temporary pine structures or in later ones of brick. "Air-conditioned" relief from summer's heat was provided by the architectural design of roof and wall.

Summer guests remembered the hibiscus in brilliant pinks, the poinsettias roof-high, and rows of blooming potted plants across the wide verandas. Poinsettias grew so profusely they were cut for huge bouquets. The tennis courts and terraces were bordered by lush green lawns. "The most attractive of mission compounds so far" was its description by Dr. and Mrs. Charles E. Maddry on their world tour in 1936. Winter visitors, however, did not fare so well, for the severe cold brought problems of heating, and by necessity clothes were worn by the layers.

Associations in Wuchow were pleasant and satisfying as the Beddoes became a part of community life. Often guests at the British Consulate up the river, the whole family enjoyed Western-world conversations and association. While the adults took part in the tennis matches, the children frolicked in games on the green lawns. Then would come the elaborate serving of the British tea in the beautiful garden setting.

Dr. Beddoe became active in the Rotary Club, and it was a tribute to him and to his work when the Rotarians subscribed the entire cost of the building of the Ha-Ching ward at the hospital. This expensive facility provided treatment of the dread hookworm disease, prevalent among women of the area.

"Yet not distressed . . . ."

Paul's words and experience provided strength and courage as the Beddoes faced yet another ordeal. When he was a young student in Dallas, Robert Beddoe was the victim of a laboratory explosion which injured one eye. Specialists over a period of years had provided treatment to sustain the sight but eventually the reckoning came. The hospital was going well—but his eye was getting worse. In fact it became so bad that it was necessary for Robert to go to Matilda Hospital in Hong Kong for further treatment. There he had to remain for many weeks in a darkened room.

As imperative as was the rest, the long period of inactivity only added to Robert's impatience and frustration at a critical time of hospital expansion and evangelistic demands. Finally, there was no alternative. Surgery was the only hope of saving his vision. The tropical sun had taken its toll, often causing ulcers on the eyeball. That meant not merely the laying down of duties for a time, but leaving them altogether. The surgery could only be performed in the States.

So in 1925, the family returned to Dallas, where two operations were performed by Dr. E. P. Carey, renowned eye specialist. After a long convalescence, Dr. Beddoe was able to go into private practice and requested that his and Mrs. Beddoe's salaries from the Foreign Mission Board be discontinued.

Some day the Beddoes hoped to return to China. In the meantime, they bought a home in Dallas where Dr. Beddoe became the doctor for the Ford Plant, with an office nearby for private practice. Mary Frances and Addie B. became American school girls, graduating from Woodrow Wilson High School in 1930. How quickly these busy years went by. Speaking schedules, church activities, summer assembly programs, Baptist Conventions both state and national—all claimed their time.

What was happening in Wuchow during these days? Ben Rowland supplied news of Wuchow and of conditions in China. In the spring of 1925, Dr. Sun Yat-sen, father of the Republic, died at Peking. The mantle of leadership fell on his disciple, Generalissimo Chiang Kai-shek. With his band of student troops he put down constant revolts, those students to become army leaders in later years. Uniting the country under the Nationalist Government, Chiang subsequently took action against the Communists. "But while the Nationalist Government was strengthening its position, Communists were also consolidating theirs. Within two years, the Red Army had multiplied its members ten times and had become a formidable weapon, its members being politically educated as well as thoroughly trained in military affairs. . . ." [1]

---

[1] Tsui Chi, *op. cit.*, p. 302.

In 1931, a "Chinese Soviet Republic was established with its government at the town of Jui-Chin, on the southeastern border of Kiangsi." The threat of Communism was always present, until the Japanese struck in 1937.

By 1933 the Beddoes were well settled in Dallas, happy in their home and church, in the medical practice, and with the news that came from Addie B. and Mary Frances in college at Mary Hardin-Baylor in Belton, Texas. There was plenty of work, both medical and preaching, to keep Robert busy.

But it was not to be. "Is there a doctor available—for Wuchow?" came the call from the Southern Baptist Mission Board in Louisville. Dr. Leavell was seriously ill and had to leave his work in the hospital. Urgently needed was a skilled surgeon, an able administrator for Stout Memorial Hospital. There was need, too, for someone to supervise the school and the evangelistic work both in the local church and at out-stations. There was no time for language study, nor for training in local dialect. This was an emergency.

It was Dr. John Lake, emeritus missionary from North China, who suggested that Dr. Robert Beddoe be interviewed on the matter of returning to Wuchow. Late in 1933 an article by Charles E. Maddry, secretary of the Foreign Mission Board, appeared in *The Commission* under the title, "God Has a Man for Every Crisis," and with it a picture of Dr. Beddoe.

So once again it was time to listen to farewell sermons, to sail for China. This time farewells were triply hard. At 51 one knows what one is getting into—the romance is tempered by realism. And leaving behind a wife and college-age daughters does not come easily. But for Robert this was God's calling and there was no turning back.

By February, 1934, contrary to medical advice that he remain close to eye specialists, Robert Beddoe was back in

China. His travel and one year's salary had been subscribed by his home church, Gaston Avenue in Dallas—no small undertaking in those depression years.

Soon after his return to Stout Memorial, Dr. Beddoe opened the doors of the hospital to private physicians of good standing. Although presenting some problems, this policy created an improvement in general attitude of the public. Later that spring, a dark room was fitted up for developing X-ray films, since Chinese patients were coming long distances for this service. Many patients came from British and American gun boats anchored in the river. In describing those "six almost-happy months" when his family was apart, Dr. Beddoe wrote of the expansion and the extension of clinical and hospital services to the thousands coming in from the strife-torn countryside.

Another matter Dr. Beddoe noted on his return to Wuchow was that the plumbing system of the hospital was so inadequate that water for all purposes had to be carried from the river by coolies. At once a message from the South China Mission was sent to the Foreign Mission Board requesting money for modern installations. The project was promoted enthusiastically by Texas Woman's Missionary Union with Dr. Beddoe's mother serving as the efficient executive secretary.

The next urgent need was equipment for eye, ear, nose, and throat work, which would cost approximately $1,000. Hospital finances would not permit expenditure for such costly instruments. Again, it was Gaston Avenue friends who provided for this need. In careful dispatches, Robert Beddoe expressed gratitude to friends of Gaston Avenue, Dallas, for the receipt of a suction and ether-vapor machine, the "last word and exactly what we needed." This was to be the nucleus for the eye clinic, a facility of long-range planning and of imperative need. Since there was no trained specialist in this field, the hospital sent their bright young doctor, O. F.

Robert Beddoe at 51, taken just before
he returned to China in 1933.

Stout Memorial Hospital, Wuchow. *Foreign Mission Board photo.*

Nurses and their charges at Stout Memorial.

Leung, to Canton for post-graduate study under Dr. C. A. Hayes, Baptist medical missionary.

Next on the list of needs was a refrigerator, necessary for the safeguarding of biological products, such as diphtheria, tetanus, cholera, and other antitoxins, vaccines, and serums. But the most pressing and important need was the early appointment of a well-equipped surgeon to give his life and talents to medical missions in China.

What was it like—to be on a hospital staff in China in 1934? Dr. Beddoe described a typical day: "The daily operation of the hospital is absorbingly interesting. After an early breakfast, the day starts at seven-thirty with chapel service. Then ward rounds precede patients' breakfast which, Chinese fashion, is served at nine o'clock. Special patients begin to arrive, keeping several doctors busy. At ten o'clock, we do our surgery, operating practically every day. Bells are ringing calling nurses, doctors, messengers. Letters from local foreigners and others arrive, requiring attention. Visitors call, telephones ring, telegrams frequently arrive, and things hum for several hours. During this time, crowds begin to gather at the out-clinic. At eleven, the hospital evangelist can be heard preaching to the waiting patients. At twelve, the clinic patients are seen rapidly as possible. Immediately after lunch, there are classes for the nurses and for the students in our girls' school. The night rounds and behold, it is time for supper! What evenings are free from meetings I spend in the office with correspondence; then one final look at any very sick patients, and I am off to bed. But that does not end the day, for very often there comes the cry of a newly arrived bit of humanity; and, frequently, I awaken in the night to stroll through the wards or to sit under the tropical stars to think out and pray through some problem or new plan."

There, under the stars, too, he wondered how things were in Texas. Louella would have to tell him every detail of the

girls' commencement activities. It was wise for her to remain
in the States for their graduation from Mary Hardin-Baylor,
and to help them in securing teaching positions. Just think of
Addie being an instructor in French and art at Oklahoma
Baptist University! And Mary Frances, teaching home eco-
nomics in Texas. How would they make out separated from
each other? Well, they were on their way now.

On September 3, 1934, Mrs. Beddoe sailed on the S. S.
President Hoover from Los Angeles to Hong Kong where Dr.
Beddoe met her. Together at last, they began the most sig-
nificant years of their missionary work.

When Mrs. Beddoe arrived in Wuchow, October 1, 1934,
to take charge of the department of evangelism in the hospital, Dr. Beddoe wrote home: "Things began to happen, the
transformation, a marvel and a joy to behold. . . . New interest spread throughout the staff and was felt everywhere
among the patients." During the first three months after her
return, two hundred and seventy-nine religious services were
held, and eight thousand and seventy-three tracts were carefully distributed.

Together again—back in China—with all the changes since
that first "slow boat" over in 1909. Much had happened
since they combined missionary careers and family years—a
long time ago in Yingtak. Always remembering the tiny
grave under the green bamboo on one side of the Pacific and
two daughters on the other side, Robert and Louella were
resolute in their teamship, their need for each other.

What lay ahead for these two veterans?

On the far horizons, the rumblings of war; just over the
hill, civil revolution; pervading all was the Red menace in
threatening workers' strikes, infiltration into schools, and
there was also Russian occupation of some missionary homes.

"We are troubled on every side, yet not distressed; we are
perplexed, but not in despair" (II Cor. 4:8).

In their future there was work to do, there were dreams to dream, there were prayers to be answered. At home there were college students preparing to come to China. A pastor-teacher, Baker James Cauthen, was ready now for language study. And a doctor was on the way from Tennessee.

7

Help Arrives

OVER and over again, and especially during the times of fatigue and the threat of lessening vision, Dr. Beddoe had pleaded for help. This urgent request to the Foreign Mission Board which he had tapped out so many times in the last ten years on the worn and familiar keys of his old typewriter was at long last answered. On September 6, 1935, Bill Wallace sailed from San Francisco for China.

Everyone eagerly awaited Dr. Wallace's arrival. What was he like? Would he fit in? Would he be alone, or would he bring a wife with him, the young woman who was with him at Ridgecrest? When Dr. Beddoe met the S. S. *President Coolidge* at the pier in Hong Kong, Dr. Wallace was alone—and remained alone through all the fifteen years of his life in China.

William L. Wallace came just in time. Young, vigorous, newly trained, enthusiastic and adventuresome, he was the perfect partner for Dr. Beddoe. Two days together on the West River steamer from Hong Kong to Wuchow gave the two time and mood to become acquainted, to talk of Texas and Tennessee, of the latest medical developments, of Southern Baptist policies and politics. They also talked about the land of China, of their work, and of the hospital, as they leaned on the rail of the deck, enjoying a leisure not to be had again any time soon.

On the afternoon of the second day, the older doctor— balding now, though still slim and youthful in appearance— squinted his fading blue eyes toward familiar scenes; the younger, erect, resolute, watched the unknown glide by, fascinated by all he saw. Each waited for the moment. Wuchow was built up the side of a hill from the edge of the West River —so beautiful but so vulnerable to the ominous Japanese threat. TAI CHI YOT POON—the concrete letters on the green embankment warned every citizen and visitor to "Resist the Japanese."

"There it is, Bill!" Dr. Beddoe proudly exclaimed at last, pointing toward the imposing five-story, gray building. "Stout Memorial Hospital!"

Yes, there it is! Dr. Wallace must have thought. *There is my destination, my work, my life.* Bill Wallace would end his life here.

The entire staff of the hospital—as many nurses as could be spared—and all the missionary personnel escorted the new doctor across the beautiful green lawns toward the terraces, and up those high impressive steps to the entrance of the hospital. A prayer had been answered. He had come! And on his fourth day there he performed emergency surgery which left interns and nurses excited about his skill and his new techniques as well as his winning ways.

After Dr. Wallace left Wuchow for a year's language study in Canton which would be interspersed with periodic visits to Wuchow, Dr. Beddoe sat down at his old typewriter to record his impressions, to appraise the situation, and to outline some now feasible plans for expansion to Dr. Maddry of the Foreign Mission Board.

"Dr. Wallace has been here," he wrote, "and I have observed him carefully. He is a fine boy and I believe he will eventually develop into a good man for this work. I doubt, however, that he will acquire the executive ability necessary to manage this hospital, but this, if true, may prove a blessing. since he can concentrate on the medical side of the work. . . . I feel that he will have difficulty with the language, I say this because he has no musical ear—which is necessary to hear Chinese inflections and properly reproduce what he hears. . . . However, Wallace has made a good impression on the Chinese people."

In the year following Dr. Wallace's return to Wuchow the hospital occupancy grew by 50 percent, its reputation greatly enhanced by the skillful young American doctor. "The Board made no mistake," Dr. Beddoe wrote. "He has a keen eye, a steady hand, and a good knowledge of surgical techniques."

True, the doctors did have their differences. Perhaps, if there were tension, it was because of their difference in age, background, communications. Dr. Beddoe was a strict disciplinarian, practical, decisive, and adamant about certain administrative details. Dr. Wallace was so engrossed in the constant emergency of need and so completely gave himself in the operating room that he was positively disinclined toward any administrative matters. And, too, he resented the slightest hint of pressure toward taking over any responsibility. He did not want to take any prestige from the older missionary. He just wanted to be a doctor in China.

As often happens in history, crises override personalities, to demand and hasten decisions. Wallace did not want administrative responsibility. But when the sirens shrieked through the walls of the operating room that September day in 1938, and the drone of planes could be heard above the hospital, all eyes of those assisting turned toward the surgeon. Never missing a motion, Dr. Wallace gave quick decisive orders—orders his analytical mind had worked out "just in case" of such an emergency. "Miss Luk, Dr. Leung, stay with me. The rest of you help the staff get the patients to the basement. Do as I say—we are not finished here and we certainly cannot stop."

In crisis, Dr. Wallace's full ability showed itself, not only during the Japanese air raids, but after, when he worked his way through the jammed corridors of wounded and dying. In that worst of the raids, a third of the city had been destroyed. Thousands were homeless or dead.

Mrs. Beddoe has written this fine tribute to Bill Wallace.

"If, as Peter Parker (a Congregationalist doctor) wrote a century ago, China was opened at the point of the lancet, we can truly say many hearts were opened by the skillful use of the surgeon's knife in the hands of Dr. William L. Wallace. The son of a doctor, his background and his regular attendance in the worship in God's house aided in pointing the way to a dedicated life by this young man. His arrival (in Wuchow) filled a need in the life of the superintendent, the Chinese staff, and all the station, and those helping in the various departments of work.

"Bill's witness for Christ was in his life, patterned so nearly like that of his Lord. Someone said at his first hearing of the Gospel, 'I might be a Christian if I could see one.' Those who saw Bill had the privilege of seeing the life of Christ lived among them. He was not outspoken in his witness, but in many ways manifested a real interest in the spiritual welfare of those with whom he lived and moved.

"When his turn came to conduct the morning worship in the chapel, it was usually brief and so planned as to include others. He cooperated with the preachers and Bible women in bringing as many patients and visitors as possible to the Tuesday night service designed to meet their needs. In the corridors, in the clinic, and during times when the air raid signals were common, his calm fearless attitude was a tremendous help and revealed a trust in a Higher Power.

"As a Christian physician, Bill was always accessible, answering calls way into the night when national doctors living in the building might have answered. He never hurried over his work as a doctor, but watched patiently for signs of recovery, assuring anxious relatives of a hopeful outcome. After rounds were over for the day, he was usually found in his workshop planning aids to a rapid recovery of some patient. The staff could hardly have been equal to the duties incident to the bombings without his help. How eagerly those young doctors seized upon knowledge Wallace brought direct from medical schools in the States!"

8

100 Years in China

—◆※◆—

SOUTHERN Baptist mission work in China was one hundred years old in 1935. It was time for a celebration! By the ancient calendars of this old, old world, such a milestone deserved little note. In the life and works of a missionary-minded organization, however, the Baptist centennial in China was most significant. All the way around from the States came Dr. and Mrs. Weatherspoon and Dr. and Mrs. Maddry Dr. John R. Sampey, representing the Southern Baptist Convention, gave a magnificent address the first evening, where two thousand people gathered in the auditorium and on the grounds of the Tung Shan Church in Canton. It has been said that the most advanced, most thriving of early Baptist missionary effort and influence was that first work in Canton. And it was to this first church that Chinese Baptists came to celebrate. Mrs. Beddoe was present, but a conflict detained Dr. Beddoe.

The orchestra of the Pui Ching High School played the opening number and accompanied the congregational singing of "All Hail the Power of Jesus' Name." The meeting closed with the singing of the Centennial Hymn, written by the pastor of the church for this occasion. Delegates from Shantung, Shansi, Honan, Kiangsu, Chekiang, and Kwangtung, Kwangsi, and other provinces as far away as Szechwan answered the roll call. Missionaries of the second generation included Mrs. M. T. Rankin of Canton and Mrs. Rex Ray of Wuchow. A fourth generation Chinese missionary was Miss Poon Kei-Oi, a great-granddaughter of the first preacher among the Hakkas.

At the same time (November, 1935) the medical mission section of the Chinese Medical Association met in Canton, coinciding with the centenary of Medical Mission Hospitals in China. "Re-thinking Medical Missions" was the theme for discussion.

In an article for American publication written out of this meeting Dr. Beddoe said: "After one hundred years, it is fitting that we should take stock of what has been done and what can still be done in this important department of missionary activity in China. My remarks will be restricted to the situation now existing in Southern Kwangsi as related to the Stout Memorial Hospital—the problems of this institution will doubtless be typical of those found in other parts of China."

He gave five reasons why medical missions needed rethinking:

1. The rapid increase in the number of foreign-trained Chinese physicians. "Until recent years, the mission hospitals were able to absorb most of these graduates, but the saturation point was reached and these doctors began opening offices and small private hospitals all over the country. These efforts should be encouraged. In Wuchow alone, there are (in 1936) fourteen Western-trained doctors in private practice, about half of them formerly interns in Stout Memorial. Shall our hospitals permit these doctors to bring their patients to us?"

2. The establishment of government and military hospitals

in most large centers. Under Generalissimo Chiang, great strides were made in medical advance, government hospitals established in most provinces. "We can no longer depend on local patronage to keep our wards full. My belief is that we should reach out to the untouched cities and villages without medical evangelism and that we should not delay in doing it."

3. The extraordinary improvement in communications, certainly in South China. "We should open branch dispensaries along the motor highways to be centers of healing and salvation, doubtless resulting in the establishment of many churches."

4. The enlightenment of the general public in the large centers. "A patient now requires careful examination and scientific diagnosis. The effect of this enlightenment will force us to send to the mission field only men with the very best equipment."

5. The abject ignorance of the rural population of the simplest rules of health. "This should inspire us to replan our work so as to reach these unfortunates not only with the benefits of modern medicine, but also with the spiritual healing of the Gospel. Here we have a great untouched field, and herein is found one of the most challenging opportunities of modern missions."

Thirty years later, this careful analysis is applicable to today's mission enterprises. In the simple, direct logic of a physician's notebook, here is another version of the great commission, relevant to an even more desperately plighted world. It was Dr. Beddoe's long-range idea that scholarships be given those nurses and doctors of faithful service who wanted to study further. He personally guaranteed the funds for Miss Ruth Nip of Canton, a graduate nurse of Stout Memorial, for six months of practical work in Public Health. Following this apprenticeship, she was to study further in a school of Public Health in Nanking before returning to Wuchow.

This was further proof of Dr. Beddoe's contention that national workers could and must be trained to carry on medical work. They must be taught first the simple rudiments of health and sanitation, food preservation, and simple home nursing care. Eventually they would be able to work in outlying villages, perhaps manning dispensaries in remote areas. China needed doctors and nurses desperately—now.

In planning toward expansion of medical care, an impromptu change in hospital procedure was the placing of all patients under the care of women nurses, indeed, a radical step, but one which proved very satisfactory, for the young ladies became better nurses than the boys. The head nurse of Stout Memorial became superintendent of nursing, assuming responsibility also for a training program as well as all housekeeping policies for the increasing developments.

At this time, there was another important development in the administrative department of the compound. The full administration of the annual Bible Conference was placed with the local Baptist church. Dr. Beddoe then was able to revise his plans for expansion of evangelistic effort. This was a different China, a different world from the one for which he had planned so carefully there on the rolling deck of the old *China* in 1918. In the same methodical way, his typing much improved, he wrote out in detail his forward-looking plans.

Later, he reported that fourteen trips had been made to two selected towns where thousands had been treated in free clinics, given tracts and an opportunity to hear evangelistic preaching. In the limited time available, and with the crude equipment, it was difficult to diagnose properly and treat so many. Several hundred people a day entered and left the little room, not over fourteen by twenty feet. But some good was done medically, and much was accomplished spiritually. Soon these out-station patients began to come to the hospital at Wuchow for treatment.

Centennial visitors in 1936 had brought inspiration,

pledges of cooperation—and news from home. In Dallas, the Texas centennial was in full swing, nothing like it ever. America had begun to look bright and gaudy in a post-depression fling. By November in Wuchow, the Chinese winter was on its way; the potted plants were brought inside; the bright pink hibiscus flowers were faded and curly-brown in the November crispness.

In a light-heartedness of relaxation after the last visitor had gone, the Beddoes observed their own anniversary. Could it be twenty-five years since the "wrong girl to Yingtak" had married the young bachelor doctor? Dr. Beddoe and the hospital staff planned a party surprise for her! He loved surprises —and the glisten and sparkle of lovely things, the luxury of fine food and of handsome appointments.

It had been a busy day, the evening chores yet to be done. From somewhere across the compound there was the sound of music—strangely familiar, but in an odd sort of rendition.

"Well, it *is* the wedding march." Louella smiled at the unique accordion artistry. "It must be Bill Newburn, over from the Christian and Missionary Alliance compound, but what is he doing here?"

Suddenly someone caught her by the arm, and in record time she was being escorted to the side door of the hospital, down a corridor to a beautifully decorated (and recently va-cated) ward, where Mrs. Rex Ray had draped silver-like material around a serving table and suspended silver foil ornaments from the ceiling. "Surprise! Congratulations!" and happy greetings from friends and co-workers, doctors, nurses, the staff, and from her Robert!

And there were gifts of silver, beautifully arranged for all to see, the most impressive a complete silver service. The inscription reads:

Dr. Robert E. Beddoe
Superintendent and his wife

Celebration of their Silver Anniversary
Stout Memorial Hospital, Wuchow

Slightly defaced by hasty packing on a day when "things didn't matter," it tells a wonderful story to succeeding generations of the Beddoe family.

Anniversary—then Christmas, 1936. Christmas in Wuchow was much like Christmas at home, but on a smaller scale. Someone would go up into the mountains around Wuchow to cut down a pine tree. There were exchanges of gifts, and best of all, packages from home. The Christmas program in the church offered another opportunity to tell the Chinese people the gospel message. But the days of such pleasant Christmases were nearly over.

By trans-Pacific airmail, the Beddoes wrote a long Christmas letter to their daughters, enclosing one to Dr. W. Marshall Craig and to the membership of Gaston Avenue Church in Dallas. They reported a glorious year of hard work, disappointments, blessings, triumphs. Dr. Beddoe wrote of "fine growth in patronage at the hospital and a most encouraging raising of the standard of our service. . . . This hospital is a good investment—a virile force in kingdom progress, a truly Christian and missionary institution."

Across the Baptist South this missionary call was echoed. But too late were the answers that might have changed the course of history.

For China was still in the throes of civil unrest—and both Communist and Japanese threats were growing. Between 1930 and 1934, Chiang Kai-shek could reach no decisive victory over the guerilla tactics of the Communist forces. Taking advantage of inconclusive civil wars in China, Japan marched into Manchuria. The League of Nations' failure to intercede began the long, disillusioning chain of events which spilled over into the aftermath of World War II and, at a little past mid-century point, resulted in the Korean incident.

Robert and Louella on their silver wedding
anniversary, November, 1936. *Below:* Addie B. (on the left) and
Mary Frances returned to Wuchow to visit in the
summer of 1937.

It is interesting to cite here the powerful advance of today's greatest threat to peace. "Communism, a Russian import, began in China in the early 1920's. From 1921 to 1927, the Communist Party, fed and nurtured by their comrades in Siberia, grew from fifty to sixty thousand and gained control of two million trade union workers and nine million peasants. In the days of Sun Yat-sen, they gained a voice in the government. When Chiang Kai-shek took over, he realized the dangerous nature of his alliance between his Kuomintang and the Communists; and he made a dramatic break with them. The Communists fought back, and the Generalissimo began an all-out liquidation campaign which by 1936 was nearing success. Then the Reds pulled off their famous kidnapping of the Chinese leader; and this, together with the Japanese threat, enabled them to exact a treaty of co-existence from the man who, a few days before, seemed destined to purge them from China's soil." [1]

But there were to be some happy interludes before the storms. Addie B. and Mary Frances, both school teachers now, came back for a summer's visit in 1937. In July Dr. and Mrs. Beddoe accompanied them on their return as far as Kobe aboard the *General Pershing*. As though prophetic of a world catastrophe, a typhoon of terrific force threatened the safety of all on board as the small vessel headed out to open sea.

It was like the voyage of 1918. Dr. Beddoe, the only passenger on his feet, was able to look after the others, having to climb his way about the rolling, pitching vessel. "It seemed that we could not survive, but somehow I had the calm assurance that my work was not finished and that all would be well. No fear entered my heart, but the thought came several times that the whole little family was in the same boat and that there would be no one left to mourn. . . . At dusk on Sunday, the 8th, we stood on the pier—on the very tip end as

[1]Jesse Fletcher. *Bill Wallace of China* (Nashville: Broadman Press: 1963), p. 119.

far toward America as we could get, and watched our daughters slowly leave us in an alien land. As the boat disappeared over the bulge of the sea, we turned our faces resolutely toward the East to face whatever remaining opportunities we have."

Five weeks later, Saturday, September 18, 1937, Mrs. Beddoe stopped her packing long enough to write the folks at home. War had come. Everybody was hovering anxiously for the morning and evening radio news. The Japanese had sent battleships to bomb the largest town on the big island of Hainan to the South, as well as planes to raid Tungshang in Canton. The "incident" at Peking in July, when Japanese and Chinese troops exchanged shots, had erupted to full-scale fighting.

"I do not know what I am packing for," Mrs. Beddoe wrote, "just to get out, of course—but when and where to go, these are the questions. Robert has arranged for me to evacuate with the Standard Oil people, taking some trunks in their boats should we have to leave. He hopes to remain and direct the work since he will be so greatly needed. He is an emergency expert. . . . I selected some of the best bedding, linens, and all the pictures I love, the silver, and a lot of little things. I have been running over the old letters that have accumulated in my office. One thing I treasure is a two-verse poem by Addie B. which she sent me a long time ago.

> In every life there is a power
> That moves us on toward Heaven;
> And as this force within my life,
> My Mother has been given.
>
> She taught me to believe in God
> This tie I cannot sever.
> Together we shall live someday,
> With Christ, our Lord, forever.

The next Monday the compound took part in air raid drills

and in a demonstration of emergency measures for nearby school buildings. Then they settled back into routine to wait, wondering how long it would take the Japanese to reach them.

The Japanese had determined on an all-out offensive in China in 1937. In July they captured Peking. In the fighting that ensued both Japan and China mobilized troops, but Japan's were better equipped and trained. Chiang Kai-shek moved his capital from Peking to Hankow, up the Yangtze River. But everyone could see it was a matter of time—and not much time—before Japan would control a good portion of China. She was already working on all the coastal cities.

Shanghai fell in December, 1937. Canton, China's large southern port, and Hankow would fall in October, 1938. Before the Japanese reached them in Hankow, Chiang moved the capital again up the Yangtze to Chungking where it stayed until the end of the war. The Japanese would work steadily at cutting China in two, sealing off "Free China" from any but air contact with the outside world, and from any source of supplies.

With the first bombing of Wuchow in December of 1937 the lines of patients at the Stout Memorial Hospital grew. And soon the Wuchow wounded were joined by the first of thousands of refugees fleeing before the Japanese troops with tales of terror.

Although both the mission board and the American Consul urged evacuation, particularly of women and children, the missionaries did not leave their posts. Now as never before the hospital was needed in China with its accompanying message of God's love in Jesus Christ.

During these days Louella Beddoe set herself the additional task of translating hymns into Chinese with the help of old Pastor Yu. On one of his trips into the coastal areas, Pastor Yu had been caught by the Japanese and imprisoned—the Japanese did not treat Christians kindly. But he had managed to give the guards the slip and make his way back to Wuchow.

It was the last verse of "Amazing Grace" which seemed to transform Pastor Yu's age and weakness into a glory of exultation—"When we've been there ten thousand years, Bright shining as the sun, We've no less days to sing God's praise Than when we've first begun." Frail and old, his memory fading after the ordeal of imprisonment, he lost his way one Sunday after preaching outside the city. A search was made, and he was traced by the sound of his faint voice. "I don't need a home," he was saying. "I'll soon be where I'll have a home not made with hands, eternal in the Heavens."

The hundred years of Baptist missionary work, along with the work of many other societies, had brought enlightenment and hope to ancient China. In the succeeding years, though interrupted by war, the Good News was still proclaimed by Chinese and missionary alike. Pastor Yu rests now in his heavenly home, surrounded by countless Chinese Christians.

9

For Every Crisis

THE FIRST bombs fell on Stout Memorial Hospital on September 18, 1938.

In Wuchow's first bombing the previous December, the main target had been the airport and the Chinese planes there. The Japanese came again in February, and this time they followed their bombs with machine-gun fire at anyone not under cover. In both raids the hospital had not been hit, and the only damage was windows broken by the explosion of bombs dropped nearby. There were more raids in May. The Japanese strategy was to fly over the city once with a load of bombs, disappear briefly, then return with both more bombs and machine-gun fire to mop up what they had missed the first time—buildings, vehicles, people.

On September 18, the bombers came again, just at busy noontime. There had been sufficient warning of their attack so that Chinese antiaircraft snapped in angry defiance with what seemed to be a successful counter. The planes disappeared over the brow of the cloud-covered mountain—only to return in minutes with their second devastating attack.

When the first warning signals started, people began to

gather in the basement of the hospital. At the second alarm the hospital gateman closed the iron gates, for if people delayed in getting under cover, they and the hospital would only draw more fire from the raging war in the skies. By then seven or eight hundred people were already packed body to body in the basement. Someone remembers that Pastor Leung kept a cool head in the panic. To avoid more panic and to calm the hysterical, he hit people over the head with a folded newspaper!

Upstairs, on the top floor, Dr. Bill Wallace was in the middle of a vital operation; he sent everyone to the basement but one nurse and his doctor assistant. When he heard the planes returning for the second attack, he sent them to the basement also, and he and the patient waited.

On their second run over the city the Japanese attacked the hospital. Bomb after bomb whined down into the compound, the buildings shook to their foundations with the explosions. And one bomb scored a direct hit on the hospital, landing in the middle of the huge American flag which had been painted on the roof as a safety precaution, right over the ward to which Bill Wallace had wheeled his patient. Only a miracle spared their lives. The roof had a huge gaping hole blasted in it and the whole top floor was demolished.

After it was all over Dr. Beddoe surveyed the damage and with cool calculation observed, "We can take a direct hit or even several hits on our roof and still stand. I know this building. I built it."

But for the moment there was no time for cool calculation or observation. There were the dying and wounded to attend to. Students who were rushing along the bank of the West River when the alarms sounded crowded into the nearby school building, and many were killed. Children in the kindergarten on the terrace level with the hospital clinic were led to safety by a quick-thinking teacher.

In the bombings and the fires that developed in their wake,

scores were killed. Many of the wounded and burned found their way to the hospital and stumbled up the long flight of steps trying to get treatment for their wounds. Other casualties were brought in on stretchers, while frightened hospital patients were being taken out on the backs of relatives. Gas fumes, broken glass, and crumbling walls added to the panic and misery.

When things had calmed down somewhat, there was time to protest to Washington over the bombing of U.S. property, particularly a hospital. But protests had no apparent effect. The American flag proved no deterrent to the bombers. Although Wuchow had no military installations, it was an important inland port of 78,000 population two days up the river from Hong Kong. It was the gateway to Kwangsi Province. Here too was the large Kwangsi University. When the Japanese saw that the British and French would probably become engaged in a European war, they began a series of bombings aimed especially at foreign property such as hospitals and universities. The Southern Baptist mission compound in Wuchow stood out as a special target. Dr. Beddoe felt that the bombing of the hospital was a warning to the Westerner to get out of China and the Far East.

As the war in China gained momentum and the Japanese gained ground, the missionaries foresaw the need of refugee zones and had established them early in various strategic locations. One center was set up in Wuchow. The well-organized one in Kaifeng on the Hwang Ho (Yellow River) in North China took care of thirty thousand women and children. As the Japanese moved south and west, so did the refugees—and the wounded. From September, 1937, air raids continued all over South China. From May 28 to June 14, approximately 1650 were killed in Canton and an estimated 6000 were wounded. The Japanese finally took Canton in October, 1938.

In spite of, or perhaps because of, the ruthless Japanese drive to the south, missionary endeavor gained momentum

Chungking, Szechuan
China
20 July 1940

Dear Dr. Beddoe,

The sum in cash of US$25.00 collected from
the passengers on the S/S President Pierce has been
handed to me.   As requested, the money has been placed
in the War Orphan Fund.   Enclosed please find a receipt.

Please extend to all those who contributed
toward this gift our thanks and appreciation for their
sympathy and interest.   The money they sent will support a "warphan" for a period of 21 months.

In spite of all the ruthless attacks upon
us by the enemy, we are continuing our resistance, and
shall carry on until final victory is ours.

Thank you for the prayers you are offering
for us.

I wish to take this opportunity to express
to you our appreciation of all that you and others of the
Stout Memorial Hospital are doing for our suffering people.

Yours, sincerely,

May ling Soong Chiang

(Madame Chiang Kai-shek)

Dr. Robert E. Beddoe
Hongkong

MCK-s/pc
Enclosure: receipt

among the people. Out-stations were strengthened and churches grew. The Generalissimo and Madame Chiang Kai-shek were cooperative toward all Protestant movements at this time. Madame Chiang addressed the monthly missionary meeting in Hankow on April 7, 1938, with words of encouragement:

"I wish to bring you greetings from the Generalissimo. He wishes me to tell you that he deeply appreciates the fine work which you have been doing to help our people. Please take this as a personal tribute to your courage and self-sacrificing spirit, to your valor and determination to help our people, regardless of dangers to your own persons and lives. On this point, may I say that we both feel deeply that words are inadequate to express our thanks to the whole missionary body in China, who have stood so loyally to their ground in spite of Japanese threats and abuse, and to those foreigners who have shown their sympathy with us in practical ways and who have been, and are, articulate eye-witnesses to the scandalous behavior of Japanese troops on Chinese soil."

In her talk she cited the contribution of Morrison who, with a Chinese teacher, translated the Bible while edicts from the Empress Dowager were sending guards to arrest him. "We see something heroic in the way he labored under the uncertain glimmer of an oil lamp, risking his life as his sampan traversed tortuous canals so that the masses might have the Bible in terms understandable to them. . . . Today, however, missionaries are working under even greater handicaps."

Among the valuable papers of the Beddoe collection is this letter on the preceding page from one of the world's great personalities whose influence, for a time, changed the course of history in China.

Although getting out of China in 1939 was extremely hazardous, the Beddoes managed to fly out "over the hump" via Indo-China for a year's furlough. At Oklahoma Baptist University in Shawnee, their daughter Addie B., now Mrs. Julian Choate, had not heard from her parents in a long time and was naturally worried. The war tension mounted daily with frightening reports from China increasing her anxiety. One day a car drove up to the door of her house—and her parents stood on her doorstep! They had decided to make their arrival a complete surprise, which it was to a delighted daughter.

While Dr. Beddoe was in the States, Dr. Wallace assumed responsibility for the medical work in Wuchow. And when word came to the Baptist World Alliance meeting in Atlanta that Stout Memorial and the compound had been bombed again by the Japanese, the Beddoes were distraught—and Southern Baptists were stunned and distressed. A year's furlough seemed too long when the Beddoes were needed in China. But there was also need to tell the people at home about the work in China, so they continued their speaking engagements across the South: Charleston, Jacksonville, New Orleans, Dallas, and even as far north as Carbondale, Illinois. Dr. Beddoe also enrolled in a special course in the treatment of tuberculosis at Saranac Lake Hospital, New York.

The Far Eastern crisis was soon displaced from the American newspapers by swiftly developing events in Britain, Europe, and North Africa. Suddenly, the world turned over, and in the writhings war seemed inevitable. The radio announcement of Hitler's march in 1939 into Poland confirmed the fears of war.

At Oklahoma Baptist University, Dr. Beddoe delivered a masterful address before the faculty and students in February, 1940. "Can Japan win the war?" he asked. Connecting the Asian war directly with the European struggle, he said, "America, wake up! When will we awaken to the fact that Japan already is fighting the United States and cease giving aid and comfort to our own enemies? We are supplying the things she needs and must have to continue to fight. Our exports of petroleum products to Japan jumped from $14,000,-000 in 1933 to $43,000,000 in 1937. Copper increased from $217,000 in 1932 to $19,000,000 in 1937. Scrap iron rose from 48,000 tons in 1932 to 1,898,000 tons for the first nine months of 1939. The European war has greatly intensified Japan's dependence upon the United States for many essential materials."

In a later speech before the Rotary Club in Dallas, Dr. Beddoe said, "The millions of war refugees who are starving to death could be supported in comfort on what America wastes." Further, he declared, the United States was standing by while an aggressor destroyed a great and peaceful nation that was in the making. "Through apathy," he said, "America has lost China, her greatest potential market." Pointing out that three factors—finance, manpower, and geography—determine outcomes of war, he observed with hope that Japan was unfavored in all three points. China at that time had 2,000,000 men in the field, 500,000 in reserves, and a total of 23,000,000 men of fighting age.

The year's furlough was soon over and the call of thirty-one years in China came again. At a farewell service in Gaston Avenue Baptist Church on April 28, 1940, the Beddoes spoke of their determination to resume their careers in China where they were needed now more than ever. In the congregation that morning were many faithful friends who had contributed to their support. Their daughters and their families, and other relatives, were also in the service—they more than others were aware of the dangers facing the Beddoes. They could only pray.

Although the hospital and home in Wuchow had been bombed twice and could be attacked any day, Dr. and Mrs. Beddoe headed back into the danger zone in early May, 1940. In a last interview in Shawnee, Dr. Beddoe said: "The day that Germany or the allies invade Holland, the Japanese will commence the seizure of the Dutch West Indies. To do that, they must first, of necessity, take Hong Kong, which would make our work unbearable. The Chinese would be driven inland, and our usefulness would be at an end. Missionaries in Japan-dominated territory are discriminated against, regarded as undesirables to be driven out. We would consider it wisdom to leave China by way of Burma and Mandalay, leaving our $80,000 hospital to the Japs."

From San Francisco, where Dr. Beddoe gave the 202nd address of his year's furlough, the veteran missionaries sailed on the *President Pierce* to Hong Kong. From there they planned to fly to French Indo-China and then to Chungking, the war capital. In Chungking they planned to visit Generalissimo and Madame Chiang before making the final stage of the trip by small boat down the rapids of the Foo River into the West River—the back-door route to Wuchow. In an article written just before sailing for the *Western Recorder,* Dr. Beddoe sounded happy, excited, as enthusiastic as ever. "We who are about to sail, salute you," he wrote. They were going back for "the best of their years."

The plans were changed, however, as soon as they arrived in Hong Kong. The city was flooded by a million refugees and the Japanese were threatening attack. Immediate evacuation of women and children had been ordered. Instead of trying to get to Chungking, Mrs. Beddoe went with other missionaries back to the Philippines, while Dr. Beddoe remained in Hong Kong. He hoped to get to Wuchow on foot —a nine or ten days' journey.

"One step at a time," he recounted for the *Baptist Messenger* in July, 1940. It was the only way to travel through Japanese territory. The nine or ten days' journey took weeks. The clay paths were slippery from the summer rains; he had to edge and dodge around Japanese sniper installations, sometimes hiding by day, sometimes spending the night in crude hovels. Although he was dressed like a Chinese, in the shiny black pants and shirt of the peasant, there was danger from gangs of roving Chinese bandits who took advantage of the confusion and increased numbers on the roads to attack and rob helpless travelers.

Finally he arrived in Wuchow to find the city virtually deserted by foreigners and Bill Wallace exhausted from his year of keeping the hospital going alone. His furlough was long overdue. "I will try to stick it out until he returns," wrote Dr. Beddoe; "then I expect to have a vacation if I have to go through to Tibet to get it!" This sounds just like the doctor. He himself was already gaunt from malnutrition. He had lost weight steadily since his arrival in Hong Kong on June 18. "I simply don't know what the matter is—the trousers I had made in Hong Kong can be wrapped around me halfway again. Well, I can only do the best I can and trust God for the rest. I hope things will clear up in a couple of months so Louella can get through to Wuchow."

It was September before Louella got to Wuchow. She came via Hong Kong and Canton with a party traveling by row boat, steam launch, sedan chair, and foot. She was the only woman in a party of five. On the entire trip, she remembers there was no water available, only hot rice water and hot tea. Native pineapples helped to quench their thirst. Anxiously on the lookout for robbers and enemy troops, they pressed on toward the free territory of Kwangsi Province and Wuchow.

Later, for the *Western Recorder,* she wrote: "There are now about one hundred and forty patients in the hospital, and we seem to be unable to get around with the Message. There goes the air raid alarm for the third time today. With the second signal, I shall be getting near the entrance to the basement room where my husband and I usually stop until the all clear is sounded. I suppose what we have here is nothing to compare to what is taking place in Europe."

All women will enjoy the following letter which Mrs. Beddoe wrote after unpacking boxes of clothing sent by her daughter's church, First Baptist Church of Galveston, Texas.

While visiting Mary Frances, she had helped pack those boxes; now she was in China to help unpack them.

"It has been quite cold; but since I am out so much, I hate to make up a fire at such expense just to burn with no one here. Therefore, I have waited until late afternoon when I was through running around to light the fire. I lighted it today about 4 p.m. But I put on more clothes than usual when I dressed this morning. Under my black wool dress with long sleeves, I have a wool undershirt and a jersey petticoat. On top of it and under my short coat, I have the little chenille jacket I became so attached to ever since the Maunceville women gave it to me several years ago. With two pairs of nylons, I have been quite comfortable, and it is far better than continually firing this thin heater. I do not see how the Chinese endure with so little clothing and such poor clothing.

"Among the things in the boxes, I found a lovely black cape with a Neiman-Marcus label. It just suited for throwing over my coatsuit when something more was needed. I never wore it, however, that something did not tell me I should not wear it. I hated to let it go, but it found its way to the shoulders of the old Bible woman, Sin E. Koo. But I am keeping temporarily a short navy coat that was in the boxes, and letting my sweater be used by one of them instead. We'll see how the conscience works in this case. I just love the last winter wool suit even though it has faded. During the summer, I think I shall have a sewing woman turn it for me and wear it on and on. Having given out all the warm clothing in the lot, we are now ripping up some of the dresses and making some cotton wadded garments.

"Kate (Mrs. Wood) or someone gave Dr. Beddoe a copy of 'I Walked Today Where Jesus Walked' and it fell into Walter Chan's hands. Imagine my surprise when he came to the choir practice at our house last week with one copy of it, but with a huge blackboard on which he had four parts written just by the use of figures all the way from one to seven. He is so talented. He sings any and all of the parts, directs, and does it well. He is giving studies in 'Revelation' at the morning prayer service, and we find it most beneficial. He is an interesting speaker and a lovable person. . . .

"Walter is the only preacher we have at the hospital, and the church has none at all. He had been filling in there, but they recently asked him to assume the definite responsibility. It will take a lot of praying for him with his heavy responsibility. He has asked me to give some Sunday School talks and to give some 'Reasons for Coming to Prayer-meeting' next Wednesday night.

"Two junior boys, children of our servants, held up their hands tonight at the meeting for servants saying they wanted to believe in Jesus. They (the servants) just somehow did not get off to the service at the church; but if we ring the bell and call them to a service here, they attend well."

In spite of imminent danger, evacuation from Wuchow in late 1940 was never considered. With every one of the 150 beds of the hospital filled, with the verandas crowded with in-patients, with 50 to 120 special consultations every day, and with hundreds at the free clinic, nothing short of enemy occupation would force the Beddoes' leaving. Although they were handicapped from lack of workers, and faced with difficulty in securing drugs and supplies due to coastal blockade, they were free to continue all phases of mission work. This was a golden opportunity in Kwangsi.

Dr. Beddoe wrote to Dr. Charles E. Maddry in December, 1940: "If you could be transported to Wuchow for a few days, your heart would be torn as mine is every day. Trying desperately to provide for an ever-increasing influx of patients, I have used every nook and corner, having had carpenters working the three shifts making beds, cleaning basements, and patching leaks; but still we are unable to meet the demand for space. We could use one hundred more private rooms and two hundred ward beds. Our staff are worn to a frazzle, but they cheerfully work at all hours. I have kept at the mails and wires trying to get suitable doctors. . . .

"At the end of each day I am so exhausted that I cannot sleep and every morning my feet and legs ache so I can hardly dress. Mrs. Beddoe grieves because, even with three helpers, she is unable to see all who come within our gates, so hungry and so needy for the truth."

In the spring of 1941, a signal honor was paid to Stout Memorial Hospital. At the same time, distinct commendation was given to Dr. Robert E. Beddoe, Superintendent. In impressive recognition of continuous and meritorious service, the hospital was presented with a scroll from the venerable Lin Sen, President of the Republic of China. The honor, the only one of its kind to be received by any hospital in China, amounted to a decoration by the government. The presentation service was held in the Sun Yat Sen Memorial Hall, which was filled to capacity by leaders of all commercial, civil, and military activity in Wuchow. Speeches of appreciation by ranking officials followed the presentation by General Liang, personal representative of the government. In his speech of acceptance, Dr. Beddoe reviewed briefly the history of Western medicine in the province and paid honor to the loyalty and efficiency of his staff. The ceremony was followed by a parade through the city with police and military escort. The hospital had operated without interruption despite the Sino-Japanese war and the bombing of the buildings.

In another letter to Dr. Maddry, dated May 2, 1941, Dr. Beddoe expressed apprehension for the future. "We have received only airmail since February, but some way a copy of *The Commission* came through. Both you and Wallace look good in the picture. I am beginning to get exercised over the possibility that Wallace may not get back here. I figure I am good for about twelve months more (at the outside) at the pace I am forced to go now. . . . What matters is the work.

What happens to me is unimportant. I believe that in some way God will keep this institution going."

Fortunately Dr. Wallace did return in October of 1941. Throughout 1941 tension mounted as the Japanese increased their offensives. America's involvement in the Far East appeared increasingly inevitable. The Foreign Mission Board felt it necessary to appoint a representative in Free China in the event that the Japanese in some way cut off communications between the U.S. and occupied China. Communication was already difficult and dangerous, and would become increasingly so. It was imperative that there be some way of supplying funds to personnel, some means of protecting property.

Some time in 1941, two American missionaries, one a doctor, met in a historic and secret meeting at a halfway point between Hong Kong and Wuchow, there to finalize plans and to evolve strategy. We can only imagine the drama of the ensuing conversation between Dr. M. Theron Rankin of Hong Kong, Mission Secretary for the Orient, and Dr. Robert E. Beddoe, Superintendent of Stout Memorial Hospital, Wuchow. We do know that the duties as representative of the Southern Baptist Foreign Mission Board in China, and all official papers, were transferred in mutual understanding from Dr. Rankin to Dr. Beddoe. In less than a year, Dr. Rankin was imprisoned in Stanley Prison in Hong Kong. Perhaps both he and Dr. Beddoe often read and thought about the passage, Acts 20:22, which then seemed prophetic: "And now, behold, I go bound in the spirit unto Jerusalem, not knowing the things that shall befall me . . . ."

General Liang, personal representative of the Chinese Government, presents a scroll from Lin Sen, President of the Republic of China, to Dr. Beddoe for Stout Memorial Hospital. The presentation was made at Sun Yat Sen Memorial Hall in Wuchow.

10

December 7, 1941

—◆※◆—

FOR MOST Americans, December 7 was a rather typical Sunday—the usual roast beef, apple pie dinner after church, a restful day between the excitement of Thanksgiving and Christmas vacations. The rush to get to Sunday school and church on time had settled into a quiet afternoon of listening to the radio. Suddenly, interrupting the program, the announcement came—like something from another planet: "The Japanese have bombed Pearl Harbor." Why, it was unbelievable! It was a hoax or perhaps fiction. Perhaps it was true.

Hours later, the radio voice that was to become familiar at each fireside reassured America—the voice of a strong decision, of a confident destiny. Never in the history of the world had such a typical day become one of such far-reaching madness. This was war. Everything changed. Since then, we have never retrieved the pattern of serenity in which we lived.

Over in China, Dr. Beddoe was up early that morning, sitting in the back bedroom waiting for the Don Bell news broadcast from Manila. Shock, unbelief, dismay—quickly, his thoughts traveled around the globe—Texas, Oklahoma,

Richmond, Virginia, the missionaries everywhere, the Far
East, China, Wuchow, the hospital.

For any crisis? Yes, he was needed! His logical analytical
mind began to organize, to make notes. There was much to
do, as he described in the long documentary letter dated
January 17, 1942, to the congregation at Gaston Avenue:

"In the fortunate event that this reaches you, you will know
we are all right for the present. I can say the same for only
seventeen of our China missionaries: Margie Shumate, Rex
Ray, Dr. Wallace, Baker Cauthen and family, R. L. Bausum
and family, Miss Hattie Stallings, J. R. and Mrs. Saunders,
Miss Annie Sandlin, Miss Ruth Pettigrew, Miss Kate Murray,
Miss Grace Stribling, and Miss Addie Cox—the last three
being at Chengchow. Wilson Fielder had just gotten to
Shanghai and Dr. Rankin to Hongkong. Miss Auris Pender,
Rankin, Miss Dodson, Mr. Quick, and the Wards are in
Hongkong. Mr. Quick had just been operated on there for
appendicitis. Dr. and Mrs. Hayes, Miss Lydia Greene, Dr.
Miller (just arrived), F. T. Woodward, and A. R. Gallimore
were caught in Canton. Rumors say these are all right. I have
no news whatever of other missionaries in occupied parts of
the country.

"When the news broke early December 8th, I immediately
started taking over the position of acting treasurer for all
China. I have worked constantly at this ever since. Finding I
could not cash drafts on the Board because they are drawn
on 'E. P. Buxton, Foreign Mission Board' and not on any
bank, I cabled the Board, and at last funds are flowing in by
cable. Meantime, I had numerous telegrams from missionaries in distress because their funds were tied up in Hongkong. The hospital had built up a reserve for such a con-
tingency, and I was able to carry on for the three weeks until
the Board got into action. I had to make journals and ledgers
—ruling and lining them by hand, for the printing business
here has practically stopped. What I had to evolve, out of a

clear sky, was a system of books for fifteen types of funds and five stations, as well as accounts for individual missionaries. It has taken a lot of time answering cablegrams from the Board and telegrams from the missionaries. I have lost twenty pounds in the process and what hair I have left is graying rapidly. If I ever have the joy of seeing you again, you need not be surprised to see me with a luxurious head of hair, for I may have to wear a wig to keep from catching fresh cold every few days!

"Through it all we both have been fairly well, though neither can sleep more than a few hours. The economic situation is exceedingly grave, so serious that an upheaval may break any moment. This may put us all in danger. Unless our country shows some sort of offensive plan soon, there is no saying what may happen.

"It would take a more gifted writer to picture the effect of the gift to our Chinese workers' Christmas. By orders of the Board, each Chinese worker received a straight gift of $75 with an additional $75 for wife and each child over fifteen and $50 for children under fifteen. One preacher's wife was so grateful that she and her children lined up, faced America, and chanted 'much thanks American sisters and brothers' while tears streamed from her. Cost of living is now two thousand above normal. The merest scrap of cloth is hoarded like gold. I wish I could be at home for a few days to thrill our Convention with a description of this thing. The figures above represent Chinese currency.

"The hospital moves along smoothly—all keeping busy. We are completely cut off from medical supplies, but I succeeded in getting a large order (seventy cases) over the lines by chartered plane just a month before things broke. So, we can carry on for some months yet. After that I don't know what we will do.

"Please get in touch with my folks so they will know we are all right. . . . Hope my Christmas greeting cable reached you. But if not, some of my dear friends at least remembered us while eating grapefruit. My! for a luscious one right now! To dear Gaston say I love them and covet their prayers."

Cablegrams record the events of the critical months following Pearl Harbor, but no graphically cryptic words could describe the anxiety, the weight of responsibility, the fears, the dilemmas of decision to be made each day involving so many lives.

December 21, 1941:
Foreign Mission Board, Richmond, Virginia
  Wire funds Bank of China reply anxious. Beddoe

December 27, 1942:
  Started sending runners December 8. Direct information. Canton missionaries all right. Indirect information believe Hong Kong, Macao missionaries well treated. Robert E. Beddoe

January 4 and 16, 1942: Foreign Mission Bulletin from letters
  Very sorry I could give no definite information about our missionaries in Hong Kong. Mr. Quick of Kweilin was in Matilda Hospital following operation when trouble broke. Dr. Rankin, Misses Dodson and Pender, Mr. Quick, and Wards caught in Hong Kong—learned through Chinese from Hong Kong who said all foreigners and Christians were taken to Shameen Island, fingerprinted and permitted to return to their usual duties and residences—with certain restrictions.—I learn that Wilson Fielder was caught in Shanghai. We have had no word from Shanghai except that all American and British property there has been taken over. . . . I am trying to arrange to get the fourteen missionaries together this summer. Have asked for a straw vote. I think we should push right ahead with a worthy program, especially evangelistic.—I think every available Chinese evangelist should be engaged to help in this campaign and

adequately paid and otherwise supported. The fourteen missionaries are Margie Schumate, Dr. Wallace, Rex Ray, Beddoes, Bausums, Cauthens, Miss Stallings, Saunders, Miss Sandlin, Miss Pettigrew. Robert E Beddoe

January 29, 1942
Direct contact Rankin and others (Hong Kong) well. Hayes (Canton) and others fed by Christians. Perfecting method send Hayes funds. Expect Galloway (Macao) news soon. Robert E. Beddoe

February 11, 1942
Direct contact Rankin and others still well treated. Rankin appeals south enlarged program West China. Direct contact Williams others (Shanghai) all right. Schools there as usual. Robert E. Beddoe

February 21, 1942: Radiogram via Chinese Government Station, Chungking, relayed by official listening post, Ventura, California: Mrs. Julian Choate, Shawnee, Oklahoma
Nearly two months and no letters to or from you yet. This is our only inconvenience. We have all in abundance, plenty of work to absorb us. Long may Old Glory wave! Mother

February 27, 1942
Foreign Mission Board, Richmond, Virginia: Cablegram:
Galloway suffering privations. Regret report Rankin's party confined Stanley Prison with insufficient food. Need prayers under crushing responsibility. Robert E. Beddoe

April 11, 1942
Foreign Mission Board, Richmond, Virginia: Cablegram:
American escaped Hong Kong concentration camp declares Rankin and party in good health March 19. Robert E. Beddoe

March 28, 1942: Transmitted by Chinese International Broadcasting Company, Chungking:
Mrs. Julian Choate, Shawnee, Oklahoma
Terrible to have no word from you, but happy to hear

Frances and granddaughter all right. Cable us any important news of Julian and Lamar. We are still all right. Unbounded love. Robert E. Beddoe

May 7, 1942:
Foreign Mission Board, Richmond
  72 British and Americans repatriated April 11 evidently included all Baptist and boat missionaries in Canton area. Robert E. Beddoe

May 16, 1942: Radiogram transmitted by Chinese International Broadcasting Service:
  Beddoes well, duties exacting, numerous responsibilities in connection with Foreign Mission relief funds—$50,000.

June, 1942
Foreign Mission Board, Richmond
  Our Soochow, Kunshaw, Wusih and Chefoo missionaries reached Shanghai for repatriation. Seventeen missionaries in Free China pushing work valiantly. Caring for fresh waves of refugees. Estimate relief need balance of year, $50,000. Chenchow reports large refugee school. Many conversions, $25,000 estimated relief needs. Robert E. Beddoe

With this assumption of the full responsibility for Southern Baptist personnel and properties, Dr. Beddoe's duties increased tremendously. He was able to secure an English-speaking typist to help with the added correspondence and records of the office. But it soon became evident that Kweilin was more advantageous for the office than Wuchow. It was further inland and away from Japanese occupied area, on the railroad, and had an airfield. At the same time the hospital in Kweilin desperately needed a head, and Dr. Beddoe was already trying to run it from Wuchow. The move, however, would entail a critical decision about the hospital in Wuchow. Stout Memorial's unbroken history of service from 1904 must go on—under the direction of a younger man. Yet Dr. Wallace was reluctant, as he had been all along, to take any administrative duties. He had consistently refused to take over any running of the hospital, except when Dr. Beddoe had been home on furlough in 1939–40.

Dr. Beddoe was both puzzled and hurt, feeling the younger man was not willing to bear his share of the load. Yet he loved Bill Wallace and respected his tremendous surgical ability.

"Bill, I don't understand your attitude."

"Dr. Beddoe, I will never accept the superintendency of this hospital as long as you are in China. It's hard to put my feelings into words, but I see this as your hospital. You built it, you saved it. You've given your life here. I don't believe this hospital should be taken from you."

Suddenly Bill's consistent refusal became clear to the older man. It was loyalty, sometimes a long-lost word between friends, that dictated the younger doctor's reaction. Later, as he told his wife about the conversation, Robert Beddoe wept.[1]

The two men worked out an arrangement whereby Bill Wallace would be temporary superintendent of Stout Memorial only for the emergency. When the emergency was over, Robert Beddoe would return to take up his duties as administrator of the hospital. Bill Wallace knew he could never run the hospital like Dr. Beddoe—and so did Robert Beddoe. But it would work out.

Bill's loyalty to Robert Beddoe, to Stout Memorial and to the work for which God had called him, kept the hospital intact throughout the terrible months of war that were yet to come. When the Japanese made their big thrust into south and west China in 1944, Bill Wallace did not leave Wuchow until the last possible minute before the Japanese marched into the city. When he did, he went with the whole staff and as much equipment as possible on board three cargo boats

---

[1]Fletcher, *op. cit.*, p. 77.

which had been waiting for them, tied up at the wharf of the river. "Stout Memorial would not die . . . it would move, but it would not die." Through the terrible days ahead, Bill Wallace's leadership and sacrifice kept his staff alive and serving the myriad refugees and wounded they encountered. And in 1945, after V-J Day, staff and equipment returned to the buildings in Wuchow.

Eventually Bill Wallace would give his life for his Lord and for the people he loved in Wuchow, cut down by the Communists. But in the Wallace Memorial Hospital in Korea, dedicated in 1968, both Bill Wallace and Stout Memorial Hospital live on.

It was 1943 when the Beddoes moved into the Southern Baptist mission compound in Kweilin which was staffed by Dr. and Mrs. Baker James Cauthen. Along with the medical duties which were numerous, the headquarters work continued without let-up. In fact both were increasing because of the refugee problem and because of the many missionaries brought to Kweilin by Air Force planes to wait for a chance to get out of China.

In the spring of 1943 a mission meeting was held in Kweilin. It turned out to be the last one, although they could not know it then. It was a triumphant gathering in spite of the few numbers and the general anxiety of the war.

The airfield at Kweilin had been built by the Chinese, and modernized in 1938–39 under the direction of General Claire Chennault who was then teaching Chinese how to fly and trying to form an air force. In 1941 he organized the American Volunteer group. Back in the States very little was known about this remarkable group of American flyers who fought so valiantly in China before and immediately after Pearl Harbor. Chennault pioneered the use of small fighter planes, and continually outfought the Japanese, even though his small force of planes was outnumbered in every battle, often by seven or more to one, and his men were hampered by lack of supplies, spare parts, even repair tools for their planes.

In their seven months of existence the American Volunteer Group fighters—Flying Tigers as the American press nicknamed them—shot down 199 Japanese planes and reduced enemy forces on the Burma Road to half their original strength. Enthusiastic words from the Generalissimo acclaimed these flyers with his famous toast: "I hope to celebrate with you in Tokyo." Madame Chiang added tribute: "With or without your wings, you are my angels."

One description of the Flying Tigers says of them: "They destroyed scores of Jap planes on the ground; they responded to calls from the British for help to protect supply lines and bases; they tore into transports and sank watercraft with no thought of monetary reward."

In 1942 Chennault was recalled to active duty with the U.S. Air Force and the American Volunteer Group was changed to the China Air Task Force. Still he had a difficult, almost impossible, time getting supplies. He begged and begged for new planes, for spare parts for his old ones. "Give us planes and we'll blast the Japs out of the sky. Give us just one bomber." By the time he was listened to, it was almost too late.

The U.S. Air Force contingent that was sent to Kweilin under Major Otte in 1942–1943 found no room for a headquarters until the Southern Baptists opened their compound. "When the boys came," Mrs. Beddoe remembers, "things livened up a bit." The Foreign Mission Board had cabled Kweilin, "Spare nothing in your ministry to the USAF."

The atmosphere of the mission compound seemed to dispel the anxieties and homesickness of the flyers. When on occasion they all got together for a meal or an evening of fun and refreshments, for both missionaries and military men it was like being home. How the Beddoes enjoyed the songfests in their cottage! The good old American music could be heard out at the airport.

Christmas 1943 was one to remember—the roast pig one. The airbase chefs in their white aprons arranged an elaborate meal, as Christmasy as possible. The doctor, looking his age now, played the piano for dear life, his fingers limbering up to the old favorites and managing to pick out the new tunes as the boys sang. For awhile it was possible to forget the war, the streaming throngs of refugees, the wounded and the dying, the responsibilities of leadership.

The Sunday church services were also moments of respite. Held sometimes in the compound chapel and sometimes on the base, they were attended by both American and Chinese soldiers and many English-speaking refugees. Lt. Clarence White from Oklahoma led the singing with Dr. Beddoe at the piano. Dr. Cauthen or Dr. Nichols would preach, and sometimes Mrs. Cauthen helped with the music.

But it was never possible to forget the war for long. The Japanese were pushing closer to Kwangsi Province and to Kweilin. And by radio it was possible to keep up with the war in Europe. Every morning Dr. Beddoe set his watch by Big Ben booming over the BBC from London. Casualties were heavy in the icy mud of the Battle of the Bulge. From Allied positions on Sicily and in southern Italy all roads led to Rome in 1944, while heavy bombardments attacked the Siegfried Line that winter. And there was a possibility that China might not be able to continue fighting. The Japanese, aware of Allied preparations in the Far East, opened an offensive to capture Assam Province and to sever the Ledo Road, the Hump Air Line, and the Assam-Bengal railway. In the South Pacific, war stalked from island to island—the Solomons, the Gilberts, the Marshalls, the Carolines and Marianas.

And all the time gold stars were falling on America.

11

He Who Began A Good Work

"ROBERT, it's only a matter of days now until the enemy will overrun all this area and we must retreat. My orders are to arrange for your start back to the States. Sorry, but total baggage is limited to thirty-five pounds per person."

Major Otte brought the word to Robert Beddoe in September, 1944. The Japanese were making what would be their last attempt to overrun China, and before they were stopped they would completely separate Free China from overland access to the rest of the world.

As the jeep jolted along the rutted blacktop road out to the airport, the doctor took one last look at Kweilin in its "flat valley of rice paddies among the black limestone ice-cream-cone peaks in Kwangsi Province." [1] Toward the southeast was Wuchow with its little mound under the green bamboo. Refugees continued their silent trudge along the road. Since 1909, except for brief respites of illness and further study, China had been his home. He could scarcely remember himself as a debonair young medic of thirty-five years ago. The

[1] Claire L. Chennault, *Way of a Fighter* (New York: G. P. Putnam's Sons, 1949), p. 186.

grand adventure was but another casualty of war to be passed over in the confusion of the times.

They were driving up to the airport now with the American flag waving over the buildings. Major Otte kept up the conversation, covering the tension and finality of the last goodbye. They both knew that soon the Japanese flag would fly over the airport at Kweilin, that the mission compound back in the city would probably not be there the next time they came to Kweilin—if there ever were a "next time." And who knew what lay ahead, even if by some miracle China's forces managed to beat back the powerful Japanese? China was still divided; communism, Chinese style, was still a threat, ready to take over China if the opportunity came.

In the Air Force plane flying to Kunming, Robert Beddoe realized he was more than tired, he was completely spent. These years since Pearl Harbor had taken their toll—administration of all mission funds for the South China Mission, responsibility for the safety of both missionaries and mission properties, helping missionaries of other denominations in their leaving China—not to mention the medical and refugee work that so drained the emotions.

"Conditions locally are none too good," he had written home back in April. "I am worried beyond endurance about four of our precious missionaries who seem to have been caught by the enemy in the neighborhood of Chengchow, Honan, and Mrs. Beddoe is far from well.

"It has seemed that the burden could no longer be borne. Actually, that is true. I cannot bear the burden. But, thank God for His unspeakable gift of a burden-bearer. O, if we could only learn to turn to Him at all times—how many sleepless hours would be turned into peace and rest. . . .

"It is my fond hope that God may permit me to return to my own country before the end. Perhaps He wills otherwise."

Now it seemed that God would grant that wish.

All other foreigners in Kweilin, except the Air Force boys,

had already left. Soon even the Air Force would be gone. Louella was waiting in Kunming and together they would fly out "over the hump" to India. And then there would be the matter of getting home. No, his responsibilities were not over yet. Eloise Cauthen was seriously ill and would require a great deal of care on the trip home. She and Baker James and the children were waiting in India, and home was still a long way off, across the dangerous Pacific.

After the flight to India in the China Navigation plane, the Beddoes with the Cauthens and other missionaries secured passage on a U.S. Navy Transport ship which would take them through Japanese-infested waters to San Diego Naval Base. Eloise Cauthen was put in the ship's hospital and the two Cauthen children were separated from their father because the men were on the opposite side of the ship from the women and children. The Beddoes and others helped Dr. Cauthen look after his children.

Since the ship was sailing through unfriendly waters, and was in constant danger of attack, all passengers had to wear their life-preservers at all times. In addition, the women were required to wear trousers or slacks so as to be ready to get into life boats. This kind of dress was a "first and only" for Mrs. Beddoe, and is recalled now with some amusement by the Beddoe daughters and granddaughters.

Thinking about home as they approached the States, Dr. Beddoe remembered a long newsy letter from Dr. John Wesley Raley, president of Oklahoma Baptist University, which had heartened him earlier that year. On Founder's Day, 1944, the OBU Board of Trustees had voted that the "honorary Doctor of Laws degree be conferred on Dr. Robert E. Beddoe, of Wuchow and Kweilin, China, at the Commencement exercises on May 26." The degree had been awarded him in absentia (Addie B. had received the diploma for her father). There had also been an invitation to preach the Baccalaureate sermon at the First Baptist Church in Shawnee

The pressures of war were telling on the Beddoes before they left Kweilin in 1944.

The Wuchow Baptist Church was bombed out by Japanese air raids. With Dr. Beddoe (left) inspecting the church after the war, are Drs. M. T. Rankin and Baker J. Cauthen. Later the church was rebuilt as a one-story building (below). *Foreign Mission Board photo.*

on the 20th of May, 1944. Perhaps the invitation would hold for 1945.

The voyage was at last safely over. For the Beddoes, home was to be Galveston, Texas, where Mary Frances (Mrs. Lamar Ross) and her family lived. Soon they were engaged in a full schedule of speaking for all sorts of gatherings. People were eager for a first-hand interpretation of Far Eastern developments. Everywhere, Dr. Beddoe made a plea for better understanding between American and China. "America will do well to cultivate China," he said before the Kiwanis Club in Fort Worth in early 1945, "for China is a peace-loving nation with unlimited commercial possibilities. China, however, needs regeneration in order to clear out dangerous trends, to put her on the road to better living, and to fit her to occupy her place among nations."

At the OBU Baccalaureate in 1945 he spoke not about China specifically but about God's great gift to the world: "Let There Be Light." In Louisville, Kentucky, he stated his firm belief that the future peace of the world was largely dependent upon friendly relations between China and the United States. He quoted Napoleon's prophetic words, "Let China sleep, for when she wakes the world will tremble." In Albuquerque, in San Antonio, in Baton Rouge, in Texas City, Galveston, Oklahoma City and Amarillo, he marshalled the cause of Christian enterprises around the world and pled for the interests of Christian education at home.

Even though the war seemed to be going against China and for Japan on the mainland of China, in the Pacific Japan was being pushed back toward home from island to island. Then in January, 1945, a convoy of American trucks and material from India crossed the Burma-China frontier, and supplies reached China by land for the first time in three years. The Allies had succeeded in flying 46,000 tons of goods over the hump into China before the Burma Road was open to traffic —that herculean project built under fire. General Gordon

Stillwell had been able to provide rough training and basic equipment for thirty-five Chinese divisions in his training centers in Yunan Province. He was succeeded by Major General Albert C. Wedemeyer who worked well with Generalissimo Chiang Kai-shek. Together they continued to fight the Japanese to the best of their combined men and abilities.

In April, 1945, General Douglas MacArthur and Admiral Nimitz directed final operations in the Pacific against the Japanese who were amassing an army of two million for the defense of their homeland.

In July, while President Truman, Prime Minister Churchill, and Marshal Stalin conferred at Potsdam, a test bomb was detonated in the New Mexico desert. In extreme secrecy, President Truman was informed of the results. On August 6, at 10:20 A.M., he announced that a B20 bomber had dropped one atomic bomb on the Japanese city of Hiroshima sixteen hours before. On August 9, a second bomb was dropped at Nagasaki.

The world has never been the same.

Robert Beddoe was 63 on September 9, 1945. But he could not think of retiring yet. He was anxious and impatient to return to China and Stout Memorial Hospital—as he and Dr. Wallace had agreed he would "after the emergency." He sailed from Houston on December 10, the first missionary to embark for the Orient from a Texas port. His baggage allotment consisted mainly of medical supplies, vitamins, and sulfa drugs—and a gasoline pump for the water system of the Hospital. He sailed alone: Mrs. Beddoe was not permitted to return at this time.

A letter written at sea on Christmas Eve, 1945, brought reassurance to family and friends in Galveston, Dallas, and Shawnee. He was happy and well, glad to be on his way back to China. Later he wrote that he had arrived in Wuchow in time to supervise the distribution of two large packing cases of used clothing which the Galveston church had shipped. "There are serious housing problems for returning missionaries. . . . With so much of our property all over China destroyed, those of us who have reached this country are at a loss to know how to handle the situation. I shall probably have to live in a boat, if they are available. . . .

"My visit to Kweilin showed me that the Lord has something yet for me to do. When I walked in on that faithful group of thirty Baptists, men and women who had lost every personal possession yet were holding a meeting of the local Baptist Association, the speaker stopped, all stood up and gathered around me, some crying. I was truly inspired. That has given me courage."

In Wuchow, "the hospital building still stood, strong and stoic, but the interior and grounds were in shambles" when Bill Wallace and his staff had returned in September, 1945. Jesse Fletcher, in his book *Bill Wallace of China,* describes the cleaning, the salvaging, the restoration, and the crude but ingenious methods of disinfecting and sanitation as well as the improvised generator for electric power set up and supervised by Dr. Wallace—and all at a time of a serious epidemic of cholera. But Stout Memorial Hospital was open again and doing business by the time Dr. Beddoe arrived early in 1946. Soon after, Bill Wallace left for furlough.

It was a new day in China. This was evident from reports of the Leung Kwong Baptist Convention meeting in Canton where Graves Theological Seminary had made outstanding contribution to Baptist missions. With the rising economy, great cities would be built in China. Eugene Hill has described the strong spiritual currents of postwar China where a million Baptists might have been organized, had not the Communists disrupted the work.

In late 1946, Dr. M. Theron Rankin, who had been released from prison in 1945 and was now executive secretary of the Foreign Mission Board, and Dr. Baker James Cauthen, secretary for the Orient of the Board, were in Wuchow for a much-needed visit to the missionaries and to the remnants of the once thriving mission compound. They brought with them, according to Dr. Beddoe, no secretarial aura, rather, a deep concern and an anxiety to be about their responsibilities; both preached in Chinese as effectively as they did in English. The meeting house was in ruins; there was no pastor and little prospect for one, but the little flock had held together.

And the little Chinese church there on main street of Wuchow was beginning to thrive. Mrs. Beddoe had arrived to join Dr. Beddoe for their last tour of duty. This was to be their most difficult work. There was an oppressive sadness about the days, a wistful wonder about the future. Everybody felt it. The landscape was still scarred by war, and in the mission compound only a few flowers bloomed of the many that had once been so carefully tended. The church building had been bombed and was still in ruins, the piano splintered, the church equipment badly damaged.

At the announcement of an approaching wedding within the church circle, the strain of heaviness gave way to momentary happiness. The Beddoes with their penchant for making the most out of every light-hearted interlude entered into enthusiastic plans with the bride, who was on the staff of the hospital, and the groom, a second-generation doctor.

Quickly Mrs. Beddoe assumed the role of bridal consultant, arranging decorations and improvising—some way, somehow —a bride's dress. What ingenuity was required where nothing could be bought and no luxuries were available! How could she manage? Then she remembered her tucked-away-for-an emergency nightgown! It was white satin, tissue-wrapped in the bottom of her trunk. Someone had given it to her a long time ago. Out of some yardage of white net which she had on hand she managed a jacket to go over the gown, and there was enough for a bridal veil. The effect was lovely and quite flattering to the bride. Not to be stymied at this point, she arranged a bridal bouquet of home-grown calla lilies, so beautifully perfect, but so soon wilted in the August heat.

The Chinese pastor officiated. Dr. Beddoe played the wedding march on the little folding organ from the mission.

The following letter of June, 1947, is both worthy of publication and important in the sequence of this story. It was directed to the South China Mission. In it Robert Beddoe looked into the future as he contemplated his nearing retirement.

"Practical experience on the mission field," he wrote, "an understanding of the Chinese people, and observation of the post-war situation in China, with other considerations, combine in forming certain fixed ideas of what should be the medical missions policy of our Mission and Board. Purely as a matter of record, and not because I have the misconception that my opinions will influence either you or the Board, I wish to state very briefly some of these opinions.

"All will admit that the political situation in China is precarious. It appears that these three eventualities are possible:

1) The Communists may be overcome, annihilated, or otherwise liquidated.

2) The Communists may overcome and take control of the government.

3) Some sort of compromise may be effected.

"How will this affect the medical program of the Board?

"Should civil peace come after liquidation of the Communists, it is my opinion that the Chinese government will, just as soon as possible, take over the control of all foreign institutions (e.g., hospitals) in the country. I mean by that, all such institutions will have to be operated by Chinese *in fact.*

"Chinese Baptists are well established as a denomination. For more than one hundred years, foreigners have guided

Above: Dr. and Mrs. Beddoe just before they left China for the last time in 1947. *Below:* The Beddoes helped this young couple with their wedding, and Mrs. Beddoe made the bride's dress from a satin nightgown. In the picture are the William C. Newburns, Christian and Missionary Alliance missionaries in Wuchow (see page 95).

their religious life. It is past-due that foreigners should abandon any shadow of over-lordship, direct or indirect. I believe that ALL of our institutional work in China (with the single exception of, theological education) must be done through (not with) Chinese Baptist churches and collective organizations.

"Permit me this further word. Mission institutes of any nature are never justifiable UNLESS THE DIRECT IMPLEMENTATION OF THE THREE FACTORS OF THE GREAT COMMISSION IS THE FIRST AND PRIMARY OBJECTIVE. That is my platform and has always been. I believe it needs to be constantly kept in mind and emphasized especially in medical and educational institutions."

This urging to turn the work over to the Chinese was never more needed. But in the light of future events it was already too late to save either institutions or the church in China.

By now, Dr. Beddoe had organized and directed the immediate restoration of the mission station, including the hospital; and he had encouraged and inspired old and new friends in South China. He felt his usefulness was limited. The torch must be passed to another generation, but one just as dedicated to the "new world" as he had been to the world that was in the first decades of the century.

At a South China Mission meeting in Canton in July, 1947, a motion was presented by Dr. Bill Wallace (just returned from furlough) and passed unanimously, requesting Dr. and Mrs. Beddoe to postpone their retirement, if their health permitted. Cited were many reasons, among them the phenomenal contribution which Dr. Beddoe had made to medical missions in China and the tremendous advantage of its continuation, and Mrs. Beddoe's outstanding evangelistic work in the church and hospital. All agreed that it was a thrilling time to be in China and that "this was the best mission meeting in forty years."

The response was dated July 12, 1947, and addressed to Miss Ruth Ford, secretary for South China Mission. There could be no turning back from the step just taken.

"I have been writing Drs. Rankin and Cauthen for eighteen months that this summer is the last I can spend in South China," Dr. Beddoe wrote. "Of course, we could stay on a few months, but I am definite in my conviction that it is right for me to leave at this time.

"How deeply I regret the fact that my retirement carries with it that of Mrs. Beddoe, even she does not know. She is the real missionary of this family!

"Because I knew it would cause me some embarrassment, and for other reasons, I sent a request that no vote be taken on this question, as affecting me.

"I think missionaries should retire from the foreign field at sixty-five, and I know that I should.

"The step we are taking is a hard one and would only be harder by delay.

"If you have the opportunity, please convey to the Mission our love and appreciation. Somehow, I feel that I will be of more value at home than out here. Certainly our love and interest will not grow less, but greater, as we watch the progress of the work as guided by younger and better equipped hands."

And so from Hong Kong, September 9, 1947, the Beddoe story in China came to a close.

"This is my sixty-fifth birthday, and I have only one more week before starting what will likely be my last voyage across the Pacific," he wrote to Dr. Cauthen in Shanghai. "I am presuming upon your good nature to write some of my thoughts concerning medical missions, in addition to what I have written recently.

"When I again took over the Wuchow medical situation early in 1934, I found the hospital in very bad repute, and a total of twelve in-patients. Aside from reestablishing confidence in missionaries as a class, it was necessary to do something radical about the hospital.

"Two main lines of action were decided: (1) to emphasize direct evangelism by announcing the policy to have the same number of full-time evangelists on the staff as doctors, and (2) to start medical itineration. Both were done—on faith—and the results you know. The two most promising out-stations of our diminishing work in the Wuchow area (Cheung Muk and Ha Ching) were greatly strengthened by and through the work of medical itinerating bands sent out by the hospital. About that time, in speaking before the China Medical Association in Shanghai, I said we should reverse the traditional ranch call 'come and get it' and 'take it to them.' At this stage in our work, with well-equipped government hospitals already established in every country, I think medical itinerating presents our golden opportunity."

Leaving China for the last time on September 19 and scheduled to arrive in Los Angeles on October 10, Dr. Beddoe was back at his favorite sea-voyage pastime, writing out his careful plans for the future of medical missions to Dr. Rankin in Richmond, Dr. Cauthen in Shanghai, Dr. Raley at OBU. These were letters of logistics, rather than of emotion and farewell. There was still work to do. He even began to write about a Baptist College, possibly in Hong Kong, a dream of all the missionaries.

In a strange destiny, the Beddoes came to OBU. Here in this campus atmosphere, he who had begun a good work, gave from his store of experience and of his fine, active mind the professional stature required for Dr. Raley's newest dream —a school of social service to be affiliated with the University. From their frequent conversations over the years, Dr. Raley had sensed the mission philosophy of this dedicated doctor; more and more he was impressed with the logic of Dr. Beddoe's mission orientation suggestions. Through reams of correspondence across the Pacific, and during the heavy schedule of 1947, these two developed a working plan for the establishment of a University Nursing Program and a School of Hospital Service-Administration. Certainly, they concurred in the concept that church schools like OBU should lead out in such humanitarian services. OBU was ideal for such a launching base.

By 1949, these ideas had been established into a definite curriculum. Extensive consultations with the American College of Hospital Administrators, with the Joint Committee on Education, and with Dr. A. C. Bachmeyer, Dean of the Division of Biological Sciences and Director of Clinics, University of Chicago, were necessary before definite commitments could be made. It was necessary also for Dr. Beddoe to reacquaint himself with American medical practice, regulations, and the requirements for entrance examinations.

Oklahoma Baptists, beginning a serious expansion into hospital services, were soon filling their posts with Dr. Beddoe's students. The nursing school, Southern Baptists' first accredited collegiate program, was very attractive. There was the beginning, too, of a department of linguistic Oriental studies, although there seemed to be only slight interest in this ambitious project. Dr. Beddoe strongly advocated a "short course," a three-month's study in basic medicine, as practical and useful to all mission volunteers. He suggested, too, a bookkeeping course. Such fundamentals of business knowledge would be invaluable to every missionary and would increase immeasurably the general efficiency in business-budget matters on the field. The whole idea had endless possibilities, and premature as it might have seemed then, it has since been proved worthy and significant. Regarding the Hospital Administration School, he wrote to Dr. Raley, "It is a tremendous program, so big in fact, that even yet, I have hardly compassed it in my thoughts—the opportunity to influence young people."

Thus began a happy relationship between OBU and the mission field. The Beddoe home, a modest cottage two blocks from the campus, became a favorite student stop, especially for those Orientals directed to OBU by alumni on the Far Eastern field. Here, too, the faculty responded to the gracious Beddoe hospitality, including delightful Chinese cuisine and the experience of eating with chop sticks. Jasmine tea was served with meals in proper Chinese style—no sugar, no lemon; to have served it with either would have been an insult to the Chinese, Dr. Beddoe felt. Evenings there spent with fascinating stories of people and places and the recounting of unbelievable and far-away occasions were highlights of the school year. No evening, of course, was ever complete without some singing with Dr. Beddoe at the piano. Each day now he practiced, going through stacks of classics—Mozart and Beethoven sonatas, the Chopin favorites—at long last unpacked.

It was here, too, that the frail Dr. Rankin came to visit. Many will remember his reluctance to speak of his prison ordeal, but rather of his burning desire to live—and to work in China.

A significant and gratifying letter, addressed to Dr. and Mrs. Robert E. Beddoe, was put into their mail box at 201 W. Midland, Shawnee, dated October 22, 1948. It was signed by M. Theron Rankin. "Dear Friends," he wrote.

"Pursuant to the understanding which we have had with you, the Foreign Mission Board took action yesterday to transfer you to the status of emeritus missionaries of our Board, as of October 1, 1948.

"In the light of my personal knowledge and association with the services which you rendered in China as missionaries of our Board, anything I might attempt to say to express appreciation of the Board and of myself personally of your services would be wholly inadequate. I do want to say, however, that we are grateful not only for what you have done in

Dr. John W. Raley, President of Oklahoma
Baptist University, with Dr. Beddoe in 1940.

Dr. M. Theron Rankin and Dr. Beddoe talk over China affairs
at Ridgecrest Assembly. *Photo by Marjorie Moore.*

China, but what you are doing now and will continue to do here at home. I know full well that this change in classification will have no effect on your services in behalf of world missions."

Personally, the Beddoes were happy, but they grew more and more anxious about world conditions as they listened to broadcast bulletins from China. "We will live to regret this day," Dr. Beddoe had prophesied, when Russia turned Manchuria and captured war materials over to the Chinese Reds. The Communists were gaining time to prepare for further conquest. By late 1948 there was no doubt. "Despite last ditch efforts by Chiang Kai-shek to correct corruption within his own ranks, deal with devastating inflation, and stem the tide of defecting commanders, the Red Dragon began to devour the land." [2] Chiang Kai-shek and the nation's capitol moved to Formosa in early 1949. The last hope for negotiations had gone with the Communist demand for unconditional surrender. The missionaries were caught in conflicting tides, Wuchow remaining the last Southern Baptist station in all China still unoccupied by the Reds. By Thanksgiving, 1949, the station, Stout Memorial Hospital, and the three Baptist missionaries were behind the Bamboo Curtain. Since then, mostly silence. One got out early in 1950. A second in 1951. But Bill Wallace died in February, 1951, in a Communist cell.

What has happened to Stout Memorial Hospital? A leak in the Bamboo Curtain lets us know that it is still a hospital— The Working Man's Hospital.

Then came the crisis of midsummer 1950—the Korean incident. By Christmas, the Chinese were at war with the United Nations, with America. Indeed, the prophecy had come true, the 1945 plea to cultivate friendship with China had been completely ignored.

---
[2]Fletcher, *op. cit.*, p. 120.

Speaking to the Lions Club in Shawnee, March, 1949, Dr. Beddoe said, "For years we have taken pride in our American way of life and its superiority to all others. But now, once more, it is in danger. And we have turned our back on our one great friendly power in the world. By withdrawing our support from the Chinese government, the U.S. forfeited one-fourth of the world's population to the Communist movement." He spoke with fright and dismay of the growing dominance of the Soviet Union in the Orient. "As China goes, so goes the world," he told the Shawnee Rotarians in another speech.

There were times when the world could almost be forgotten in the delight of campus occasions where everybody seemed young and happy, in the association with returning veterans who expanded OBU's facilities and required new buildings. Moments of music Dr. Beddoe never missed. How he loved the recitals, the concerts, the magnificent choir at the Baptist church! There was time now for his own compositions. One he dedicated to the persecuted Chinese Christians, a lovely hymn, "Let Not Your Heart Be Troubled."

There was also the stimulation of faculty groups, committee meetings, American campus conversation. A favorite speaker for all occasions, Dr. Beddoe maintained a rigorous schedule for both university and town occasions. In carrying on their field work for the Foreign Mission Board, Dr. and Mrs. Beddoe were an unbeatable team, filling numerous engagements for mission schools, rallies, and church study groups. To this real home in America, the children and grandchildren came to visit often, brightening the days and dispelling the memories of lonely ones in China.

They were "Americans again," in sort of a dream life of normalcy, living on a quiet street with real neighbors, in a typical town in the Midwest. What a handsome couple they were, and what an asset to church, college, and social circles.

Almost dapper and debonair again, Dr. Beddoe enjoyed the good things he had almost forgotten, new clothes, good food, good fellowship in clubs, the Medical Society. Always proud of Louella, he had encouraged her on every furlough to adapt herself to American ways again. This time he insisted that she take up the American custom of going to the beauty shop for regular care of her beautiful silver hair. She must shop, too. Her clothes must be in fashion, American style—and she wore them well.

Trips to Oklahoma City afforded the advantage of concert and opera; at the University there was always good music. When it was necessary to be interviewed by Medical Boards and accrediting agencies, or to confer with curriculum committees, frequent trips were made to Chicago, or Cleveland— perhaps to Washington or New York. He took every advantage to know his country better. Once in New York, he was given a real "welcome" by *Oklahoma,* the popular, post-war "sing-along" musical, still playing, after 20 years, to capacity houses. Accompanied by Dr. Raley on this trip, they both came home singing the tunes to everybody on the campus who would listen.

Home at last—and a "good work" to continue. Since 1944, Major Otte's jeep had come a long way.

Let Not Your Heart Be Troubled

Dedicated to the persecuted Christians in China

R. E. B.

R. E. BEDDOE

1. In-to the darkness of sin and shame Bringing sal-va-tion, the blest Saviour
2. Come unto Him tho' you're sad within, Tho' you are wear-y and burdened with
3. There is pro-vi-ded a cure for care; The Ho-ly Spir-it this truth will de-

came. Tho' you are sin-ful, downhearted, de-ject-ed, O, trust Him com-
sin. Je-sus has promised to lift all your bur-dens, O, come to the
clare. O-pen your heart to His gen-tle in-struc-tion, And peace will be

REFRAIN

plete-ly your life to re-claim. In-to each dark-ened life He'll come
Sav-iour, new life to be-gin.
yours that is be-yond compare. Let not your heart be trou - bled,

Bring-ing the light of God's ho-ly Son. Dy-ing He'll save you,
Ye trust in God, trust al-so in me. Mansions of light in

Liv-ing He'll keep you. Trust Him to lead you safe-ly back home.
Hea-ven I'm build-ing; There with your Lord you ev-er will be.

Used by permission of Broadman Press.

12

"American Gentleman, Friend of China"

——✣——

AT OBU, the telephone in the president's house rang at four-thirty in the morning, January 18, 1952, and over it, the familiar voice of a neighbor-doctor: "Come at once. Dr. Beddoe has just slipped away."

It was dawn for Robert Beddoe after three score years and ten. He had been so happy the evening before as he and Mrs. Beddoe had prepared a Chinese meal for some of the students and faculty. Later, he played two numbers, the music still there on the piano—Kreisler's "The Old Refrain" and Bach's "Jesu, Joy of Man's Desiring."

Morning brought friends, faculty, students, and telegrams by the score. By the time the daughters arrived with their families, the home was a beautiful bower on this cold January day. Loving tributes were expressed two days later in an unusual afternoon service in Shawnee. His pastor Dr. Harold Lindsey, an old friend the Rev. J. E. Kirk, and Dr. John W. Raley, officiated at the service. Dr. Raley spoke of Dr. Beddoe's contribution to world missions in a first career. He cited renewed vigor and influence in a second career—on the campus, where developing plans for Hospital Service-Administration were well under way, and where all the medical files were in perfect order.

The organ music was quiet with lingering beauty and dignity. Clarence White, the Oklahoma Air Force lieutenant once stationed at Kweilin, sang a number he had often sung in those anxious days of the war—"Be Still My Soul" to the "Finlandia" melody by Sibelius.

The funeral service was held the next day in Gaston Avenue Church, Dallas, Robert Beddoe's home church. His old friend, Dr. J. Howard Williams, President of Southwestern Baptist Theological Seminary, Fort Worth, was in charge. Home to Texas, the "young doctor" returned from that uncommon career and dramatic adventure he had begun in China forty-three years before.

With his passing, Oklahoma Baptist University suffered a unique loss, for in so few years of his new career he had brought a priceless something to campus. Cosmopolitan in attitude, knowledgeable about the cross currents of contemporary history, he had lifted student eyes to the boundless horizons of the world. Many remember him best for the treasures of his personality, that bit of sparkle, that dash of the debonair, that edge of subtle humor—but all submerged at times in the depths of a tired, aching heart. For his distinctive contribution to the University stature during those critical years, and for his vigilant concern for all students in his role of University physician; most of all, for his "plans for the future" in the development of humanitarian concepts, the University is ever indebted.

The messages, condolences, and tributes were filed in careful order. These came from both hemispheres, from doctors and hospitals, denominational officials, medical associations, pastors and people, professors and universities. Both in the States and in China, memorial occasions were arranged, while resolutions and appreciation came from many sources.

From Dr. M. Theron Rankin, Secretary of Foreign Mission

Board, came a hand-written letter, one of the first:

"After I received the telegram, I sat in my room and let my memories run back in China, back to Wuchow and Canton, and on up through the years to the present. How good it is to think also of the thousands who share in the kind of heritage that Robert Beddoe has left, a heritage that spreads over a large part of the world."

"Dr. Beddoe's life was so full of music and healing and witnessing and administering for Christ and souls," wrote Miss Ruth Pettigrew from New Territories, China. "I can never forget what he meant to us in Free China after Pearl Harbor. How he must be enjoying the celestial music of Heaven."

Dr. Baker James Cauthen from his post as secretary for the Orient of the Foreign Mission Board, also recalled the days of stress in China. "My thoughts turned back to the unforgettable time when he shared his convictions with me about the primacy of preaching the gospel of Christ before I went to China. Then I found myself traveling again with him across the country of Kwangtung Province and walking on the compound of Kweilin—Now, he is sharing with Bill Wallace a fellowship sublime."

Frank Otte, now a retired Air Force Major, summed up Dr. Beddoe's life in a fitting military salute. "To me, he was always a stout soldier of the Cross and one who now has earned his terminal leave. . . . As I sit here, the many China scenes which we shared come back to me; especially impressive was the way he took, in Christian stride, all the destruction of his life work. We, who were military men at the time, had to steel ourselves against this (and our then-defeat) or otherwise our courage would have buckled."

Dr. E. C. Routh, religious journalist, wrote to Mrs. Beddoe, "He was one of our most faithful missionaries—and his ministry was made more effective because of your unfailing re-enforcement."

From one of his China colleagues, W. B. Glass, who was also the father of Eloise Cauthen, came this tribute: "I always admired Dr. Beddoe for his fine Christian spirit and loyalty to the missionary call and purpose."

Two unusual tributes to Robert Earl Beddoe were written in 1964 at the request of his grandson Marc Ross who needed material for a high school term paper assignment. The first came from Dr. W. W. Thornton, Professor of History at Oklahoma Baptist University.

"It was during the war days in the 1940's when I dropped into the president's office at Oklahoma Baptist University to confer with President Raley about a problem relating to my department. 'Let me read you a letter,' he said, 'which has just arrived from war-torn China.' It was a message from Dr. Robert E. Beddoe, missionary in charge of the Stout Memorial Hospital at Wuchow, China. It gave a vivid picture of conditions then prevailing in that unhappy land. Between the lines, one could read a story of faith and courage on the front lines of Baptist missionary endeavor. In the thick of it was Dr. Beddoe.

"That was my introduction to the man who was to become my friend and colleague during the post-war years. As Director of the Hospital Service Administration (after 1948), Dr. Beddoe brought to this post a wealth of experience and wisdom in administering hospitals. The training program which he developed at OBU bore excellent fruit. Among the men who trained under Dr. Beddoe's supervision is the present administrator of the Baptist Memorial Hospital in Oklahoma City, Mr. J. L. Henry.

"It was while he was living in Shawnee that Dr. Beddoe learned of the martyrdom of Dr. William L. Wallace, the young man who had taken over the work at Stout Memorial Hospital. When Dr. Beddoe made the announcement to the congregation of the First Baptist Church on a Sunday morning in 1951, he was visibly shaken. The Communists had uprooted and destroyed most of the work which represented Robert Beddoe's life and had murdered the man who was trying to carry on. But that morning Dr. Beddoe expressed faith in the God who sees not merely the tangible things of life, but rather the indestructible things of the spirit. In that crisis, the faith of a great servant of God shone forth. I felt that I saw the true Robert Beddoe, the man who, with his Lord, could see ultimate victory in the midst of seeming defeat."

The other tribute was written by Dr. John W. Raley, Chancellor of Oklahoma Baptist University.

"Dr. Beddoe will long be remembered by those who worked with him as a man of many interests and of great curiosity.

"A blend of medicine and missions gave him his life pursuit, while music inspired his soul and relieved the harshness of the many tasks confronting him in missionary enterprises.

"An executive by nature and experience, he developed an objectivity in his analysis of the total Christian problem in its socio-political and economic setting and attacked his phase of the problem with scientific skill and intuitive understanding.

"Dr. Beddoe was in large measure a crusader and a perfectionist. He fought hard for any cause he espoused, and he fought with precision facts.

"I recall the many conferences we had relating to the establishing of the Hospital Service-Administration Department of OBU with keen appreciation of his scientific analysis of the needs and his stubborn insistence on going beyond initial requirements to make the program the best in America. That the department has held its place as the first collegiate nursing program in Oklahoma and the only accredited program in Southern Baptists' colleges and universities can be credited directly to the high standards set up by its first director, Dr. Robert E. Beddoe.

"All in all, I can say that I am richer in my life because of his friendship, and that he and the lovely Mrs. Beddoe reflected great honor on OBU by making the campus their home for his climax task.

"A great human being, a dedicated doctor and missionary, an artist in appreciation of the good and the beautiful, he lives on in the memories of his friends."

For the record, an obituary is written, but these are only facts. As Robert's Aunt Bertha (Mrs. Hal F. Buckner) said, "A doctor's life is not put in words." The fragments here and there tell the real story. In the box with all the clippings, the family pictures, the mementoes for the grandchildren, here is a bit of his writing, words and music—for remembrance. Like many keepsakes, yellowed and frayed, this little sheet of notepaper is to be cherished as another fragment of the story. This is a sketch of a song—a hymn—he had begun. Laid aside for awhile, only this was written, the pencilled melody along crooked lines of the staff.

Sunset comes to every sorrow
Through the sunrise of his grace;
Brightness comes to each tomorrow
With a glimpse of his dear face.

Perhaps some day it will be finished—another memory of this unusual combination of a man—musician, physician, missionary.

Among all the tributes from the great and small, the near and the far, one is a summation of a personality once known to a little Chinese girl, a refugee whom he befriended on a cold, rainy day during the war. In an unusual maturity and a rare wisdom she expressed the highest tribute of all: the doctor in an old world was the "American gentleman, friend of China."

EPILOGUE

Westward to the East

◆

From western horizons, the Pan American plane eased onto the new runway of Hong Kong's Kai Tak Airport, that stupendous engineering feat that moved the mountains into the sea. Set down at night from an altitude of almost six miles at six hundred miles an hour, one is immediately encircled by that many-jewelled, many-splendored tiara—fabulous, fantastic Hong Kong, 1963. That was the beginning of our modern missionary journey. For eleven days and nights, Dr. Raley and I were caught up in the incomparable spell of mission enterprises.

Forty-five years before, a promising young Dallas doctor and his family had sighted this same landing. From another world, in a carefully written diary, he set his course in the stream of Chinese history. "Hong Kong! We will soon be there! But for war conditions we could easily reach the harbor tonight. But we must idle along so as to reach it by daylight tomorrow. As I write now, we are steaming along at about eleven miles per hour. The sea is calm and beautiful—as indeed it has been ever since we left Japan. It is April 2, 1918, and 10:00 in the morning. All is well.

"What are my thoughts as we approach the port where we will leave the old *China*? Do I have to steel myself to meet the varied experiences that will come to me during the seven years which begin when we land on Chinese soil two days from this morning? Can I be absolutely honest with myself and say that there is no regret, no sorrow, no turning back in my thoughts? I am exceedingly happy to say that I find nothing of this in my heart. I would love to be an ordinary person and enjoy the pleasures that come to the average successful head of a family. I would love to be a homebuilder and see my children grow up to the responsibilities of life in my own beloved country, surrounded by friends and loved ones and the influences of good churches and schools. I would love to acquire a bit of this world's goods and have a plot of ground, a house, a home which I could call my own. . . . I would like to attain a position of power and influence in my community and be recognized and patronized as the best doctor or surgeon in the country. These things, and many others, call to me and offer an alluring pathway . . . but God has given me grace to disregard all of these pleasant calls . . . to turn my face to the East and return to the land where few—almost none—of these things will be found. So as I approach Hong Kong, I find that my heart has within it a great Peace; and I can say 'all is well.' The quiet sea without, the warm, bright sunlight, and the slowly but majestically moving steamer are all in harmony with the Will of God. And that is more greatly to be desired than great riches."

How different now is this little bit of China off on the rim of Asia to that he knew in 1918. As Dr. Raley and I continued our tour, we were driven on exploratory trips along the paved, but narrow roads of the New Territories to see for ourselves the lookout points just a few hundred yards away from where the Bamboo Curtain stretched from guard to guard. Beyond, lay the vast and remote stretches of mainland China, now Red China. Between our road and the guards, a narrow strip of "no man's land" largely occupied by the Hakka people is the lonely vigil of Miss Ruth Pettigrew, Southern Baptist stalwart among her beloved Chinese.

In a primitive scene, the water buffaloes padded along in the rice fields while the Hakka women, in their brown, umbrella-like fringed hats, trudged along the edged highway to the village markets with the bamboo baskets of fish and fowl, strange fruits and vegetables. Momentarily, we were intruders in an old and weary land.

Along the Baptist trails, we passed several mission points, a preaching station, and soon a modern church building of freshly painted stucco. Nearby, the brown hillsides were dotted with the burial plots of Buddhist graves, and in the hot sun were traces of paper flowers. At Aberdeen fishing village, the hopeless squalor of the boat people added another dimension to our perspective.

And then, in sharp contrast, the splendid city, Kowloon–Hong Kong! The "new" of this British Crown Colony loomed to greet us with tall skyscrapers and handsome apartment buildings, with smart shops and luxurious hotels. Here, the exploding economy of shipping from the seven seas, industrial expansion, and fashion excitement, is one of the phenomena of our time. Visitors to Hong Kong never forget the pressure of people, the three and a half million population, walking and milling all day, all night. This last stand, the remnant of an ancient culture, ninety-nine percent Chinese, clings desperately to China's shoreline and symbolizes that "golden opportunity" which Dr. Beddoe envisioned so many years ago. Embarking on that last voyage back across the Pacific in the fall of 1947, he wrote:

"The start that has been made in China is a good start, but only a start. The foundation already laid is sure and strong. Upon it can be built a shining super-structure to the glory of God. It must not be an alien building superimposed upon a secretly resentful constituency, but a native product built by, with, and through Chinese Christians. Statesmanlike planning is in order, and such planning for conquest must not overlook Hong Kong."

One wonderful night brought us nearer to the stars, guests at a dinner-party including Dr. Lam Chi-fung and members of his family, the David Wongs, and officials of Hong Kong Baptist College. From the roof-garden of the Carleton Hotel, the panorama of brilliant beauty, of light and color, transcended anything I had ever seen. The missionary pointed out the sentinels of Baptist progress in the city below. There was the hospital, white and shining and new, to be dedicated in the fall. Across the way was the new site for Hong Kong Baptist College, now with a thousand students enrolled; in 1947, it was only the challenge which Dr. Beddoe included in his dreams. Over ten thousand students are enrolled in schools operated by the Hong Kong Baptist Association. Do you see the busy thoroughfare down there? Just off it is the Baptist Building, headquarters, bookstore, and press—a launching base for Baptist expansion into China, where one-fourth of the world's population lives, and into the South Pacific. Fifteen thousand strong are the Hong Kong Baptists organized into thriving churches, the buildings already over-crowded and inadequate. And there, up in that beautiful high section, is the Baptist seminary, one of the finest facilities of contemporary building, provided by the Lottie Moon Christmas Offering.

The scope of it all, the magnitude of such humanitarian concept—even in today's unbelievable world, is difficult to express. In his "Hong Kong Report," July, 1963, Dr. Raley concluded that the missionary is in the most strategic spot of history: "I have seen the heroic proportions, which as a boy I cast for David Livingstone, clothe the missionaries in Hong Kong. These self-effacing men and women are standing in the stream of history. . . . Releasing the energy of the human spirit through education and Christianity, they give stimuli to all areas of activity, social, economic, industrial, political, educational, and religious."

*   *   *

The plane lifted. I turned to wave to our missionary hosts standing there on the upper ramp of Kai Tak. Toward home now, Westward, to the writing of a story that began with a faded picture still tucked in my purse. In so short a time it had become a symbol of that missionary march from one century to another, from one generation to another.

"Go ye, therefore . . . ." The command is still timeless. And how incalculable is the influence of even just one life lived on the mission field. It is impossible to measure the life and influence of Robert Earl Beddoe—the number of lives touched for good, the healing of bodies and souls, the men and women introduced to Jesus Christ—because he went from Texas to be a Doctor in an Old World.